Legal Action f

A grassroots anti-sexist, anti-racist
Since it began in 1982, it has focuss
advice and support to low-income
to be denied justice.

LAW combines access to a network of sympathetic lawyers, with experienced lay workers from similar backgrounds to the women using its services. Its insistence that no case is "hopeless", that something can always be done, has won LAW recognition from legal professionals, civil rights and welfare organisations, and community groups. LAW has helped prevent many injustices and set important precedents, including with the first private prosecution for rape in England, which resulted in an 11-year conviction.

International Black Women
for Wages for Housework

An independent grassroots network of Black women and other women of colour founded in 1975, which makes visible the unwaged work women do for every community and every movement for justice. In Los Angeles in 1992, they produced a Legal Defence Information Sheet "as a community resource" in the aftermath of the No Justice, No Peace rebellion. In the West Indies they have spearheaded the movement for the rights of domestic workers. In Britain they have recently launched the Asylum from Rape petition to get recognition that all sexual violence is torture and therefore grounds for asylum.

Both **IBWWFH** and **LAW** have been supporting the campaign to free the Tottenham Three and later Winston Silcott since the late 1980s. They can be contacted at

Crossroads Women's Centre
230a Kentish Town Rd, London NW5 2AB, England
Tel (0171) 482 2496 minicom/voice Fax (0171) 209 4761

Other LAW publications, all with *CROSSROADS* Books, include:

Handbook: The Child Support Act — Your Rights and How to Defend Them (3rd edition 1994)

Dossier of DSS Illegalities: Implications of the Child Support Act (1993)

Dossier: The Crown Prosecution Service and the Crime of Rape (with Women Against Rape 1995)

Clockwise: Winston aged two. Winston with mother and father. George at Vigil of miscarriage of justice campaigns outside High Court, 21 April 1997. To his right, Valerie Davis, sister of Michael of the M25 Three wrongly convicted in 1990.

Backcover photo: Vigil. Placards include Jane Dawson sentenced to nine years for stabbing her violent boyfriend in self-defence. LAW is helping with her appeal.

A Chronology of Injustice

The case for
Winston Silcott's conviction
to be overturned
by *Legal Action for Women*

Chronology compiled by
Niki Adams

Introduction by Nina Lopez-Jones

Preface by Sarina Silcriss of
International Black Women for Wages for Housework

Editor Selma James

CROSSROADS

Published January 1998 by *CROSSROADS* Books

ISBN   0 9517775 7 2
A catalogue record is available from the British Library

General editor   Selma James
Cover design   Cristel Amiss
Typing/formatting   Fanny Weed

CROSSROADS Books
Crossroads Women's Centre
PO Box 287
London NW6 5QU, England
Tel (0171) 482 2496 *voice and minicom*
Fax (0171) 209 4761

Cover: Mary Silcott with a photo of her son Winston, 1997

CONTENTS

Reception for the Silcotts at
Crossroads Women's Centre
17 July 1997

Top left to right: Niki Adams
George Irving (actor)
Jim Robinson (one of the
Bridgewater 4)

Centre: Adrian Clarke
(Winston's solicitor)

Bottom: Mary Silcott & guests

Why we are working for Winston Silcott's Release

Let us remember from where we all come
Remember who mothered you
Or drowned in your shame.

Winston Silcott

For an independent Black women's organisation like ours, it is the exception rather than the rule to take scarce time and resources to campaign for men. But we are convinced that there are compelling and urgent reasons for Black women — and everyone concerned with justice — to work for Winston Silcott's release.

Winston is best known as one of the Tottenham Three whose 1987 convictions were overturned in 1991. This case has been among the most notorious examples of how Black people have been unjustly treated by the British criminal justice system. It was the Silcotts' misfortune to live on the Broadwater Farm Estate when in the eighties it was designated as one of London's "symbolic locations" for major shifts in policing policy (see "Not an 'ordinary' conviction" below). This aggressive policing is now dominant in Britain, and has continued to engulf the Silcott family — among many others.

Winston is the only one of the Tottenham Three still in prison. The chronology demonstrates that he is not guilty of murder in the death of Anthony Smith but that he is being kept in prison for the murder of PC Blakelock. As long as he remains inside, the forces which put him there are encouraged and strengthened.

7

Winston Silcott has demonstrated sympathetic awareness of what women, beginning with his own mother, have to face. This has encouraged us to support him, in addition to supporting women unfairly convicted, and to persuade other women and men to do the same. Winston himself is known for defending others. Jim Robinson of the Bridgewater Four,[1] taking part in a roof-top protest to highlight the miscarriage of justice which had him in prison, has said publicly: ". . . that man supported me when I was in Gartree; when I went on that roof, the first man to throw me a tin of food was Winston Silcott." Winston has referred women's cases to us, and has gathered other support for them.[2]

The impact of the case on Black communities

In the same way as Black children are up to six times more likely to be excluded from schools,[3] Black men are more likely to be stopped, searched, arrested and imprisoned.[4] This is the framework of all our lives, women, children and men:

---

1 The Bridgewater Four were wrongly convicted of the murder of newspaper boy Carl Bridgewater. Michael and Vincent Hickey were both on roof protests. Michael spent 89 days on Gartree Prison roof, with the almost unanimous support of other inmates. For an account of this extraordinary organising see *Murder at the Farm*, Paul Foot, Penguin Books, 1996. Pat Molloy, the fourth man, died in prison.

2 Winston wrote to ask us to help Sara Thornton, convicted of murder when she killed her violent husband, whose mail was censored in prison. He also asked others to support her campaign, which won a re-trial and her release in 1996.

3 In 1997 the Commission for Racial Equality reported that up to 14,000 children in Britain are permanently excluded from school each year; Afro-Caribbean pupils are four to six times more likely to be excluded than their white counterparts. (*Guardian*, 24 September 1997, p.5)

4 In 1993-94, 25% of people stopped and searched by police were Black or from "ethnic minority" groups, although we are only 5% of the population. In London, it is 42% double our 20% of London's population.

branding our communities as outcast and criminal has wide implications for the treatment we receive in every sphere, from employment, to housing, to physical protection — or the lack of it as in the case of Stephen Lawrence.[5]

Getting Winston's conviction overturned will set an important precedent against this branding and the outrageous treatment it justifies and incites. It will send a message to those in authority that Black as well as other working class communities aren't prepared to be criminalised, cheated, excluded or physically attacked because of who we are.

(*Hansard*, 1 December 1994, reported in *National Association for the Care and Resettlement of Offenders newsletter "Race Policies into Action"*, January 1995) A survey of young men in custody found that 29% were Afro-Caribbean and that they come "from more stable home backgrounds, ie were less likely to have been in care, more likely to be still living at home, and they truant from school less". (*Black People and the Criminal Justice System*, Report of the NACRO Race Advisory Committee, 1986)

Afro-Caribbean people face an imprisonment rate of eight times that of white people. (Social Trends, Central Statistical Office, 1994) 38% of prisoners on remand in London are Black. (*Black People and Remand into Custody*, National Association of Probation Officers, 1989) 24% of women in prison are Black or from "ethnic minority" groups. Black and "ethnic minority" men were 18% of men in prison. (*Home Office Prison Statistics England and Wales*, 1996). Men of African and Afro-Caribbean origin serve sentences 44% longer than those of white men; African or Afro-Caribbean women were serving twice as long as white women; and Asian women had the longest sentences of all. Men of Asian descent also serve longer sentences than white men. (*The Idenikit Prisoner*, Prison Reform Trust Report, 1991). The proportion of Black people in prison has been steadily rising.

5 Teenager Stephen Lawrence was killed at a bus stop by five white racists. His murderers were never convicted in part because the police did not at first pursue them. The police let Stephen die without even giving him first aid. Some of those who attack and even kill members of Black communities go free, while the police who in this case seem to be accessories after the fact are not charged, disciplined or dismissed, and continue to draw salaries for "protecting" us . . .

Women's justice work

Injustice is a lot of work for women. Expected to care for families day in and day out, often on top of a job outside the home, it goes unremarked that it is usually women — mothers, wives, partners, sisters and other relatives and friends — who support and sustain both men and women in prisons and detention centres.[6] When people are sent down for crimes they have not committed or get longer sentences than the offences usually carry; when they are conscious of being unfairly treated and constrained by imprisonment from acting to prove it; then the work of sustaining them is even more arduous and shattering. Women far more than men are trained to keep ourselves and each other in one piece so we can continue to do this justice work: swallow hard, put your head down, and keep working. Not surprisingly, women are often the driving force of campaigns, whether or not they are prominent or even visible in them, to get loved ones out or to win justice in other ways.[7]

Black women, who must deal with the disastrous personal and social effects of racism (while on the firing line ourselves), carry a disproportionate burden of this justice work, whether or not there is a conviction. Mary Silcott related to us her experience as the mother of a boy the police have marked out to target:

---

6 Refugees and immigrants, many of whom have escaped rape and other torture, are increasingly held in detention centres or prisons; 90% are Black people. They can be held indefinitely — as long as two years in some cases — without being charged with any crime.

7 It is Mrs Doreen Lawrence, Stephen's mother, who has spearheaded the campaign to get her son's death acknowledged as a racist murder and to bring those responsible to justice. Anne Whelan, Michael Hickey's mother, and Ann Skett, Vincent Hickey's mother, spearheaded the Bridgewater Four campaign for 19 years before their convictions were overturned.

"From the age of 14 the police started on Winston. Just riding a bike without lights, and they took him to court. From that day on they never stopped. They told me that if a pin dropped anywhere in Tottenham, they're coming for him and they're going to lock him away for life or send him to the madhouse.

"We couldn't get any peace. George hardly could walk outside, they're behind him as well. When they [Winston or George] go out at night, I don't close my eye until I hear the key in the door because you always worry if they're going to come back or not. Sometimes I go to work and I'll say to Winston when I'm coming home to bring the bag for me down the road. When I come in he's not there. When I do find him, they've picked him up, locked him up, just like mice, in and out all the time. In the end they let him go, they find nothing, no charges.

"They hated to see him when he dresses up, going up the road; they'd say, 'He looks too good.' With the Blakelock case, they used to ask the young boys, 'Have you seen the best dressed man going up the road, have you seen him? Where is he?' It was just like something out of a movie. Why they hate him so I just don't know.

"Especially after Blakelock, they parked right below the window where I was living. I don't know what they were standing there for. It was like that all the time, watching us going, watching us coming. It affected the whole family.

"And all that time I had to go to work . . . I'll have to work until I drop."

What mother will not know how wounding it is not to be able to save your child from such persecution? Many mothers, Black and white, know because this experience is not so rare. What is rare is any acknowledgement, official or unofficial, of this persecution which has shown itself to be integral to the criminal justice system. When magistrates and judges hand down decisions, do any of them take account of this?

And if they don't know about it, why don't they know? It is not justice but injustice which is blindfolded.

Mary Silcott with her husband William and her son George have done the painstaking and exhausting behind-the-scenes work of going back and forth to prison and lawyers while coping with a witch-hunt (see chronology), while Mary is also holding down a job as a carer to support her family financially. The impact on the Silcotts of this toil and trouble has been enormous, wrecking among other things the older Silcotts' health and plans for the future. (The Silcotts are from the West Indian island of Montserrat. Their prospects have been further shattered by the 1997 volcanic eruptions, leaving most of the island uninhabitable; they can never return.) We have taken it upon ourselves to help sustain Mary Silcott outside since she has been central to sustaining Winston Silcott inside.

The family priority to free George's older brother has shaped his life too. His campaigning work has increased with the ill-health of his parents. It was George Silcott, the family's "front-runner" (according to Mary) who, at Winston's insistence, had to press the lawyers to get the ESDA test done, which led to having the conviction of the Tottenham Three declared "unsafe and unsatisfactory". And the work had to continue when his brother remained inside for Smith. Not many know that no-one would give a Silcott man a job, which is why Mary, despite bad diabetes, works nights and is the family's sole support.

Mary is of course no exception in doing this triple day of housework, waged work, and justice work. Women's work in movements for justice is almost always "uncounted, unhonoured and unsung".[8]

---

8 Introduction to *Strangers and Sisters: Women, Race and Immigration*, ed. with an Introduction by S. James, Falling Wall Press, Bristol 1985, p.21.

". . . while it is public knowledge trhat Black people, and particularly young Black men, are regularly harassed, falsely arrested and beaten by the police, there is rarely a mention of the women — mothers and sisters, wives and lovers — who go back and forth to courts and prisons, who organise defence committees and attend their meetings sometimes on winter nights after long days spent cleaning hospitals; or who deliver to prison cells, along with home cooking and cigarettes (and at times unwelcome words of advice), the laundered shirts, so that the accused — son, brother, husband or lover — can appear before his persecutors dressed in the community's care and support."[9]

We called a vigil with others in April 1997 outside the Bridgewater Four Appeal Court hearing to highlight other miscarriages of justice. ("Justice for the Bridgewater Four. Don't forget the others!") Some of the men taking part had trouble acknowledging what was before their very eyes, that the vigil *was* mostly women with photo-placards of campaigns for mostly men inside. It is generally hard work to get men — of any hue, class, background or persuasion — to begin to consider and acknowledge women's contribution, even though their lives depend on it.

Women were again central at a demonstration we attended with the Winston Silcott Defence Campaign in November 1997 outside the Criminal Cases Review Commission in Birmingham. Called by Action Against Injustice, it was held to support a national hunger strike and other organising by prisoners protesting their wrongful convictions, and refugees who have committed no crime (see footnote 6). Women were the ones who lobbied and got two of the Commissioners to meet with families and supporters.

Clearing the Silcott name will cut down on the horrendous burden of justice work now sapping many women's lives.

---

9 Ibid., p.20

We also have to remember that women are at the same time themselves on the receiving end of police violence. Mrs Cherry Groce in Brixton was confined to a wheelchair, and a few days later Mrs Cynthia Jarrett at Broadwater Farm lost her life, both as a result of police raids on their homes. Two major urban confrontations were sparked off by violence against these two Black mothers.

Working with Winston

From 1988, like many others, we supported the Tottenham Three Families Campaign, which in 1991 got those convictions overturned. After that, we and LAW stayed in touch with Winston, who remained in prison. Unlike the Tottenham Three, Winston's murder conviction for the death of Anthony Smith did not seem to be political, and did not get as much publicity and support: although many people knew there was an injustice, it did not seem so great; after all, Winston *had* killed Anthony Smith — and Smith was Black. Also, the Smith case was not seen in connection with the Blakelock case which has in fact dominated it. The racist component of the Smith conviction wasn't obvious until the two cases were looked at together, beginning with the screaming racism of the headlines which had shaped both cases once the Tottenham Three were found guilty. (LAW's chronology is particularly useful here.) The campaign to get Winston out fell more and more onto the shoulders of his family — who have always been the core of the Winston Silcott Defence Campaign. We worked with Mary and George, and directly with Winston.

Getting to know the Silcotts better made it easy to understand Winston's reputation as a man of principle and courage. Like others who learn the law in the course of trying to prove their innocence, and who have first-hand knowledge of how the law works in practice for people like themselves, Winston has made himself into the kind of skilled legal expert that grassroots people urgently need. We asked Winston's advice on a case we did with LAW and discuss with him initiatives we are working on. Winston has never been so overcome by his own misfortune that he is not entirely committed to helping others. He always responds promptly to letters, managing to keep organised and up to date on issues of concern to Black and other working class communities — despite the authorities breathing down his neck and trying to cut him off from the world outside. We send him regular mailings from our Centre about what we and others are doing and information we think he would find of interest. Payday Men's Network does a regular collection from their network to help with his food, books and phone cards. We write to him regularly, and visit him at Maidstone Prison in Kent.

Prison conditions

We are constantly aware of the harsh conditions imposed on Winston and other prisoners. Rules introduced in the last couple of years limit how much they can spend weekly according to how they are categorised. Winston can only spend £10. Prisoners must choose among essentials: buying phonecards and stamps to maintain contact with family, friends and legal representatives; or essential items like soap and shampoo; or food to supplement prison meals which have never been nutritious and are increasingly insubstantial. "Continental breakfasts" (e.g. a hot drink and a bread roll) have replaced hot breakfasts; and for the first time in November 1997 in Maidstone Prison sandwiches and chips replaced a hot lunch. Prisoners can buy additional food but at higher prices inside prison than outside.

Not only phonecards, stamps, toiletries and food, but also the estimated value of gifts sent by prisoners' families and friends are all deducted from his £10 allowance. In some prisons, including Maidstone, these deductions extend to books and journals. Winston has had to refuse books sent by friends because a prison officer set the price at £30, which would have wiped out his allowance for three weeks (though other prisoners have been allowed similar books for 50p).

Another measure removed entitlement of prisoners to one hour of exercise daily. Exercise time and access to sports and other facilities, so crucial to maintaining people's mental and physical health, are now at the discretion of the governor. Gym visits or recreation periods are sometimes cut to one a week. In this climate of scarcity and stress, Black prisoners are more likely to suffer.[10] For example, so-called random drug tests target some Black prisoners so frequently that they jokingly speculate whether theirs are the only names on the list!

Clearing the Silcott name

Once the Tottenham Three had been convicted, the media described Winston as an "animal", a "wild killer ape", practising "the evil eye", having a "dreadful Black visage" and have never stopped. The aim can only be to make Winston an "untouchable", cutting him off from all social sustenance and support. Even Broadwater Farm, where hundreds of working class families Black and white make their home, was written off as a "jungle".

One of the worst slanders is a Scotland Yard source (quoted in full below) saying, "You should be glad [Winston Silcott] is in jail for the sake of your mother and your sisters." To imply that Winston is a rapist promotes the most backward and crass racist stereotype of Black men as a danger to white women. We can't afford to let this go unchallenged. Such stereotypes

---

10 A report commissioned by the Home Office says, "Nearly half of the Black inmates questioned said they had been racially victimised by prison staff; 55% of Black inmates said they had experience of racial discrimination in access to facilities and activities." (*Reported and Unreported Racial Incidents in Prisons*, Oxford U. Centre for Criminological Research, 1994)

have always set up and endangered the whole Black community, including Black women. What is decisive is that *no police have publicly dissociated themselves from this racist slander.* What does this tell us about the relations top police want to have with Black communities? And if such false and vicious comments are made publicly, what lies and slanders are retailed in bars, pubs and social circles where top police, journalists and lawyers meet to eat, drink and trade gossip?

Equally malicious and racist is the police officer reported as saying that Winston ". . . extorted money as the leading muscleman of the estate . . . brave residents, many of them Asians, who tried to stop the evil racketeer had their homes firebombed." (*Daily Mirror,* 20 March 1987) Working class communities like ours haven't got the power to counter such libellous slander circulated in millions of copies. At least the Broadwater Farm Inquiry, an independent examination of the 1985 events, chaired by Lord Gifford (see below), shows all this to be a malicious lie. In the same way as the police and press invoked women's safety to cut off support for Winston, they invoked protection for Asian people to divide him as an Afro-Caribbean from his Asian neighbours.

The irony is that Asians in particular have been convicted for defending themselves, as Winston was; and have also got disproportionately long sentences, as Winston has. Satpal Ram killed one of a gang of six racists who attacked him in the restaurant where he was working. For defending his life he was convicted of murder and has already spent 10 years in prison. Injustices are harder to overcome by any community on its own. No wonder there are constant attempts to set those of us of Asian origin against those of us of African origin.

In July 1997, we held a reception to honour Mrs Silcott and her family and to help counter the media portrayal of Winston as a wild and dangerous killer. Hiding who he really is and how carefully he was brought up in a caring, religious and supportive family, has been central to demonising

him. The extremely successful and crowded event demonstrated how much support there has always been for proving
Winston's innocence. It rekindled and refocussed interest in
his case.

But we found that people, including our own network, did
not know the basic facts. We therefore asked LAW to prepare, in consultation with Winston, this chronology of events.
We had supported LAW's work on the private prosecution for
rape they had helped bring; and had witnessed their attention
to detail in preparing a case. We were confident that LAW, a
multi-racial service which takes on the cases of women dismissed by professionals with, "Nothing can be done," would
do the job that was needed: factual, thorough, precise, com-
passionate and anti-racist.

We are satisfied that this chronology of events and evidence which they have placed before the Criminal Cases Review Commission demonstrates Winston's right to his freedom and for his name to be cleared. We recommend it to all
who are, like us, concerned with justice; in supporting Winston
Silcott, we support and defend ourselves.

Sarina Silcriss
International Black Women for Wages for Housework
23 January 1998

From Winston Silcott . . .

Is it a fair trial when a family suffers because of hatred, fabrication and lies reported by the media, lies leaked by the Metropolitan Police whose only objective is to cover up the true nature of their corruption . . .

Is it a fair trial when press stigmitisation backed up by people with power and authority, influence the outcome, your fate regardless of your innocence . . .

Innocence is determined by decisions which depend on the look of the accused, skin colour, their sex and background. The present criminal justice system can only be described as a major tool that offers to cut corners to gain guilty verdicts instead of finding out or searching for the truth . . .

The Silcott family has undergone great hardship ever since the law enforcement sank its Dracula-like teeth into me . . . Regardless of all the undue persecution, my mother has shone through the smog of deceit and dirty tricks. Over the many years, through sickness, my mother has kept the family together emotionally, financially, spiritually, and has always been there for me . . . Who are the real criminals?

A criminal justice system that destroys a whole community and targets the Silcott family . . . Because the Metropolitan Police don't want to be exposed or proved wrong for another accidental-on-purpose terrible blunder. Who are the real criminals?

A mother whose love for her family and whose belief in justice keeps her strong to struggle on no matter how big a mountain of obstacles are put in her way . . .

The magical connection of womanhood has brought my mother into contact with other women who share similar experiences. The women and men who work at the Crossroads Women's Centre have held out a helping hand

to support my mother in the fight to receive belated justice
. . . people within the Crossroads Women's Centre have
aided and supported me . . . knowing that I face an uphill
struggle due to the fact that the Metropolitan Police are
doing everything possible to keep my plight out of sight out
of mind . . . The Metropolitan Police have untold taxpayers'
money at their disposal to mount their anti-Silcott
propaganda . . .

I do not proclaim myself to be an angel. I can clearly
put my hand on my heart to declare that I am NO demon or
evil man as some sections of society often love to portray. . .

There are many who need to depict me as a bogey man
to brainwash the general public and to justify my wrongful
conviction . . . I put it to you: if defending one's life is
wrong, then everyone should carry the bogey-person label.

If it wasn't for people with common sense, the farce that
holds me incarcerated would have left me to rot under the
injustice carpet . . . I thank you all who are genuinely
behind my family in their battle to prove my innocence for
murder. Self-defence is supposed to be NO offence . . . In
the unjust case used to hold me captive, the powers that be
were and are politically inspired to keep me, along with
other innocent women and men, in Her Majesty's prison.
Rather than correct a terrible wrong, the justice system is
prepared to turn a blind eye to us innocent victims. We the
wrongly convicted are an embarrassment to the criminal
justice system's status quo . . . This is why it takes people
outside of the judicial system to try and rectify many of the
miscarriages of justice cases . . . .

Sex, race, disability and sexuality are no grounds of guilt
. . . people with a criminal record and Black people can be
innocent too!

No Justice, No Peace
W. Silcott
November 1997

Summary of new evidence

The Criminal Cases Review Commission has the power to refer the case back to the Court of Appeal if they consider that there is a real possibility that the Court would regard the conviction as unsafe. There is now a substantial body of evidence before the Commission which shows that Winston Silcott acted in self-defence. This evidence includes material gathered since the original appeal proceedings, and in particular the following:

a) A statement from the doorman of the Club where the incident took place bears out that Anthony Smith, the man who died, was armed with a knife during the fight with Mr Silcott.

b) Statements from two other eyewitnesses say that Anthony Smith was armed with a knife.

c) A statement from the main prosecution witness at the trial states that, if she had been asked at trial whether it appeared to her that Winston Silcott was acting in self-defence, then she would have said that he clearly was.

d) A statement from a barrister indicates that Mr Silcott had told his solicitors that he had acted in self-defence and was advised by them to diverge from the facts. Notes made for the junior barrister also indicate that she must have known.

e) The legal test in cases where people put forward a different account before the Court of Appeal from what they put forward at the trial, has altered. The Court of Appeal in Winston Silcott's case said that rarely, if ever, would appellants be allowed to put forward a new account. However, in the

later case of Richardson, the Court said that the new accou
should be heard if there was real evidence of a miscarria
of justice.

f) Evidence that Mr Silcott's arrest and false conviction f
the murder of PC Blakelock undermined his ability to g
justice in the Smith case. The original Smith trial is mo
likely to have been prejudiced by press coverage of N
Silcott's arrest for the Blakelock murder and of th
Broadwater Farm events. Since then, racist tabloid pres
coverage has disseminated and supported the police vie
that, "guilty or not", he must stay in jail. The process of as
sessment and decision in the Smith case has been tainte
by this prevailing view.

* * * * *

As his lawyer Adrian Clarke has pointed out, *"Not only i
there substantial evidence supporting Winston Silcott'
account but, equally significantly, there is no evidenc
which goes the other way. If the evidence now availabl
had been put forward at the original trial it is difficult to se
how Winston Silcott could ever have been convicted."*

Legal Action for Women
12 February 1998

Not an "ordinary" conviction

"One Scotland Yard source said recently: 'He is an animal. I don't care if he is guilty or not. You should be glad he's in jail for the sake of your mother and your sisters.'" (Independent on Sunday, 7 August 1994)

In March 1987 Winston Silcott and two other men were convicted of the murder of PC Keith Blakelock. In 1991 the convictions were overturned as "unsafe and unsatisfactory" after scientific evidence showed that part of Mr Silcott's statement was not made by him and must have been fabricated by the police. But unlike his co-defendants, Mr Silcott was not released. He is still serving another life sentence: shortly after having been falsely charged with the murder of PC Blakelock, he was tried and convicted of the murder of Anthony Smith.

There is abundant and growing evidence that this conviction too is deeply flawed, and is maintained by a continual witch-hunt against him. Winston Silcott does not deny that he killed Anthony Smith. What he denies is the charge of murder. The evidence is mounting to prove his claim that he acted in self-defence.

There is also hard evidence that he was ill-advised and negligently represented by his lawyers, a charge the legal establishment is always reluctant to consider.

Mr Silcott has been in prison since 1985. If he is serving a sentence for Mr Smith's death, he should have been released by now. But evidence points to other reasons for Winston Silcott being kept in prison.

Of those wrongfully convicted for the murder of PC Blakelock, he is the only one who is still inside. There is abundant evidence that he is being kept there in order to justify the discredited Blakelock conviction. The police and the media together have been urging the public and the legal establishment into the view of Winston Silcott as a dangerous man who has escaped conviction for the murder of their colleague and deserves to rot in prison on whatever charge — a kind of rough and racist justice.

In every case which is proven to have been a miscarriage of justice, the police have stuck with the view that, regardless of the evidence and the verdict of the court, those wrongfully convicted were guilty. Instead of charging those responsible for the murder of PC Blakelock, the police seem determined that Mr Silcott will pay.

In March 1997 Mr Silcott's case was put in the hands of the Criminal Cases Review Commission, the body set up to look at cases where a miscarriage of justice is claimed, and decide whether or not they will be sent back to the Court of Appeal. We have urged the Commission to refer the Smith conviction to the Court of Appeal.

Unless it is looked at again, this time *taking into consideration all the facts and events in their sequence and context,* the basic questions about the case cannot be understood. These questions are:

♦ Why did Winston Silcott not raise at his trial that he acted in self-defence?

♦ Why was basic evidence which unambiguously supported this plea not brought before the court?

♦ Why didn't his lawyers make this obvious — and truthful — defence?

♦ And why are the police and media still pursuing Winston Silcott?

A racist and violent context

A major conflict between the police and Black communities raged in the early and mid-eighties in various cities and neighbourhoods. The 1983 London-wide survey by the Policy Studies Institute provides ample evidence of Black people's experience of a racist and violent police force. The police, it says, used stop-and-search powers to harass, intimidate and criminalise Black communities. This continued despite the "sus" law* having been abolished in 1981 after it was proved that "sus" was being used by the police in an illegal and racist way. Following street protests in Brixton in 1981, the *Scarman Report* made a series of recommendations to deal with police/community relations including: action against racist behaviour by police officers, close supervision of stop-and-search operations, and the immediate setting up of consultative arrangements with the community.

While acceding to such recommendations, the police leadership singled out four inner-city multi-racial neighbourhoods in London as "symbolic locations" where civil rights were to be secondary to law enforcement. Sir Kenneth Newman, Commissioner of the Metropolitan Police from 1983, also brought from the armed conflict in Northern Ireland, where he had been Chief Constable of the Royal Ulster Constabulary, policing methods such as surveillance and plastic bullets. Broadwater Farm was one of the "symbolic locations" where, superimposed on community policing — policing by consent — was confrontational policing — policing by force — which had conquered during the 1984-5 miners' strike.

An example of such policing happened just days before the Tottenham events. On 28 September 1985 in Brixton, South London, Mrs Cherry Groce was shot in her bed by a

---

* Arrest on suspicion that you intend to commit a crime.

police officer and permanently paralysed, triggering a major street confrontation. A week later, on 5 October, on the Broadwater Farm Estate in Tottenham, North London, Mrs Cynthia Jarrett died after being pushed by a police officer during a search of her home. Mrs Jarrett was 49 years old and the mother of five children, including Floyd, a founding member with (among others) Winston Silcott of the Broadwater Farm Youth Association; Michael, who made a statement supporting Winston Silcott's self-defence claim; and Patricia who was at home with her mother during the raid. Outraged by the death, the community demanded the immediate suspension of the officers involved in the search and decided to stage a sit-in in front of the police station. But while in Brixton the officer responsible was immediately suspended, in Tottenham the police refused to suspend anyone and surrounded the estate so that a planned peaceful protest could not take place.

The conflict which then erupted on Broadwater Farm resulted in the death of PC Blakelock, and was followed by a police investigation which wilfully denied legal rights to hundreds of people arrested for questioning, many of them under age. The police justified these methods by blaming community policing for the death of PC Blakelock. In *A Climate of Fear: The Murder of PC Blakelock and the Case of the Tottenham Three** David Rose quotes *Police* magazine, November 1985:

"Compromise and the avoidance of confrontation only leads to disaster." (p.83)

In the same issue of *Police*, under the title "Community Policing Confuses the Force", Sir Eldon Griffiths, the parliamentary spokesman for the Police Federation, writes:

"Community policing in theory, is an unarguable public good. But it can only work where there is a comparatively

---

* Bloomsbury Publishing Ltd., 1992

settled and homogeneous community. And such is not the case in our multicultural inner-city ghettoes . . . the police must be able to respond to the challenge of violent crime and lawlessness with whatever force is required to uphold the law as Parliament makes it . . . community policing has obscured this responsibility." (p.84)

What had he done to provoke this?

In 1970 at the age of 11, Winston Silcott moved with his family to Broadwater Farm Estate. Broadwater Farm is a working class estate; at the time, about half the families were white and half people of colour, mainly of African and Afro-Caribbean descent.

The Broadwater Farm Inquiry, headed by Lord Anthony Gifford QC and conducted after the 1985 conflict, describes the living conditions of those who made their home there: structural defects, disrepair, damp, cockroach infestation, lift breakdowns, poor security, poor cleansing services, poor transport. The conditions were so bad that in 1980 the Department of the Environment considered the estate's demolition. From 1981 efforts were made by the residents and in particular the newly formed Broadwater Farm Youth Association to improve conditions, and the *Inquiry* credits them with many successes.

During the early eighties, in the years running up to the deaths of Cynthia Jarrett and Keith Blakelock, relations between the police and people living on the estate, particularly Black people, steadily deteriorated. The Broadwater Farm Estate was often subjected to saturation policing. Residents said it was like living under occupation by a hostile police force.

By the time of Anthony Smith's death in 1984, Winston Silcott had been a police target for years. Mrs Mary Silcott, a religious woman, describes how at the age of 14 (in 1974)

27

her son was stopped by the police for riding his bike without lights and how *"From that day . . . the police were on Winston's back every minute."* In 1979 he is tried for a murder he did not commit, for which he is acquitted. It is clear from looking at the evidence that he should not have been prosecuted in the first place. But the police seemed determined to get him. He is stopped or arrested at least once a week. Once he was picked up three days in a row.

To be subject to this treatment often, and to the threat of this treatment always, has been shown to be the fabric of life for many Black people. Charges against Black defendants, including Winston Silcott, must be seen in this context.

Winston Silcott was a founder of the multi-racial Broadwater Farm Youth Association called together in 1981 by Dolly Kiffin and others. The *Broadwater Farm Inquiry* describes the Youth Association as a turning point in bringing the estate community together. The Youth Association provided subsidised meals not only for young people but for pensioners, many of them white, and spearheaded demands for services for everyone on the estate and surrounding areas. These services included a day nursery and a number of co-operative enterprises such as a launderette and the greengrocer shop run by Winston Silcott. The June 1985 issue of the Youth Association's magazine reflects this variety: *"Services for Turkish Speaking Residents"*, *"Asian Activities At The Mothers' Project"*, *"Disabled People Start To Organise"*, *"Hairdressing Salon Opened"*. The Youth Association also led to major changes in the composition of the mainly white Tenants' Association — it voted a new committee with equal numbers of Black and white members and adopted a new constitution.

In February 1985 the achievements of the Youth Association received official recognition with the visit of Prince Charles and Princess Diana. Winston Silcott asked Diana why had she come if she wasn't bringing any jobs. Comments like this which working class people like Winston don't always have the boldness to express, must have helped shape Diana's respect for and identification with the "constituency of the rejected". But the police were furious and the tabloids implied that Diana's life had been under threat. Far from feeling threatened, she remained in touch with the Youth Association.

The *Broadwater Farm Inquiry* shows that the Youth Association and the Broadwater Farm residents generally were interested in building good relationships with the police, in particular the patrol officers. Lord Gifford says, *"We have not heard from anyone who does not want the police to do a job for the community."* (p.52) What people refused was oppressive, racist policing which did not address their concerns, as shown by a survey to prioritise violent attacks such as sexual assaults on women (84% of residents), heroin control (69%), mugging and domestic burglary (66%), racial assaults (59%). (p.162)

The *Inquiry* found deep disagreements within the police. Some local senior officers were committed to community policing. Chief Superintendent Couch described the Broadwater Farm Estate as *". . . a nice place to work on for our police officers. . . . And we worked in good co-operation with the housing department, and with Miss Kiffin, who was on the Broadwater Farm [Youth] Association."* (p.40) Others shared this view of the estate. An officer from outside Tottenham was overheard saying: *"I expected to come and see a load of rogues, villains and vagabonds, but I find the majority of the people on this estate very nice people."* (p.147)

But the estate and Youth Association did not have the support of those senior officers and other police who were hostile to community policing and to Black people. Commander Dickinson who had overall charge of the area between 1981 and May 1985 and Deputy Assistant Commissioner Richards who took over in 1985 were often provocative in their public comments on Broadwater Farm. The Association's claim that providing young people with a centre had led to a substantial fall in crime was dismissed by Commander Dickinson: *". . . it only proves that they were responsible for it in the first place . . ."* (p.44) And DAC Richards who refused to suspend the officers involved in the raid which caused Mrs Jarrett's death, viewed the estate as *"a haven for the wrongdoer"*. White residents also confirmed to the *Inquiry* the racism of many officers. A white woman after a burglary quotes a police officer: *"Oh you've had some coons breaking in, have you? I don't know why you live around here with bloody nig-nogs trying to break in to your house."* (p.51)

While Black people on the estate were getting themselves together and getting together with white residents, the police were annoyed that many residents had more confidence in the Youth Association than in the police. They were particularly annoyed that the Youth Association had refused to allow a Neighbourhood Watch scheme to be set up on the estate (which the Youth Association feared would target young Black people as *"objects of suspicion"*). The Youth Association soon became a police target.

The *Inquiry* notes that:

"Attempts at building good relations were regularly set back by the insensitive and unnecessary actions of [Special Patrol] units which enraged local youths. Haringey's Chief Executive, Roy Limb . . . described what used to happen:

"'. . . things were going quite well, all of a sudden there would be another incident on Broadwater Farm and that would damage the relationships . . . Out leapt policemen and a number of youth were detained, questioned and so on . . .'" (p.40)

"Stafford Scott, a youth worker with the Youth Association, gave a vivid picture of how the Association pressed for contact with patrolling officers, only to be confronted with two men who plainly had no intention of being community policemen . . . 'They actually kicked open

the Youth Association's door and stood with hands on hips holding truncheons, and they just looked in, in a very aggressive and antagonistic manner.'" (p.41)

Winston Silcott says:

"They [the police] used to swarm over Broadwater Farm and do what they wanted. When the Youth Association was organised . . . people started standing together and complain if something was wrong . . . If I saw a youth get arrested, I would ask him for his name and address and get a solicitor for him to inform his parents. The police tried to intimidate me, but I would stand my ground and take notes and inform the family." (*Guardian*, 25 April 1992)

Not only was Winston Silcott part of the Youth Association, he was also widely respected on the estate as someone who insisted on justice. He often attended meetings of Haringey Council's Police Sub-Committee. He has spoken about how furious the police were, labelling him a "troublemaker" when he stopped them from "making a deal" in the Sub-Committee over an incident of police violence. The community representatives on the Sub-Committee had demanded an investigation of the unprovoked beating by police officers of Danny Stewart, a local car mechanic. When Mr Silcott arrived at the meeting where this was being discussed, he found that the police were offering to take young people from the estate on a visit to Hendon Police College as a way of getting out of conducting an investigation into the beating of Mr Stewart. Mr Silcott insisted that it had to be investigated. The police said: don't listen to Silcott, he's a troublemaker. But the other community representatives agreed with him and rejected the police offer.

The police persecution of Winston Silcott was extended to his younger brother George and to the whole Silcott family. The Silcotts were threatened by the police who said they would make sure Winston got put away for life, either in a madhouse or a prison. On a number of occasions when Winston Silcott had been picked up and held at the station, the police came to search his home. Mrs Silcott relates how on one occasion the police came looking for Winston and when his father told them Winston wasn't home, they beat and kicked William Silcott, and then arrested him. Winston and William Silcott were both later released without charge. This ongoing police attack on the community led in October 1985 to the violent and tragic deaths of Mrs Jarrett and PC Blakelock, events which in turn engulfed Winston Silcott.

People who are regularly stopped, searched, racially abused, bullied and beaten know of course that they cannot rely on police for protection or justice. Their experience leads them to expect that anything they say, no matter how truthful, can be disbelieved and may be turned against them. This must tilt the scales of justice at every turn. The responses at the party where Anthony Smith was stabbed show how widely that community distrusted the police: over half of the several hundred people who were present were questioned, and most of them refused to give the police any information. Judith Young who went on to become the main prosecution witness, when first questioned said she *"did not see or hear anything unusual until the arrival of the police;"* and *"I have nothing further to say and wish to go home."* Mr Smith's friends, Wayne Jones and Renton Nelson, also initially refused to co-operate with the police. At the trial the prosecution describes the community's response to the police as a *" wall of silence,"* but tries to blame this on Mr Silcott, saying that people were scared of him. There is no evidence that people were scared of Winston Silcott. There is plenty of evidence that in that period many people were scared of the police. The police were not trusted by Black communities, or by anyone, Black or white, who had a criminal record; they felt they would be rounded up as the *"usual suspects"*: guilty until proven innocent.

Yet Winston Silcott, who had been targeted more than most, has often been condemned for not disclosing the truth to the police; condemned, that is, by those who are used to protection and respect from the police, and think that if *they* were mistakenly accused of a crime, telling the truth to the police would clear it up. It is vital that such people finally recognise the obvious: Winston Silcott was not in their position.

The lawyers' role

To find out why at his trial Mr Silcott did not make the truthful case that he acted in self-defence, and why evidence which supported this was not presented, the role of Mr Silcott's lawyers must be examined.

At the trial Judith Young, who gives a consistent account throughout, makes clear that the fight was not started by Mr Silcott, that he was attacked and seemed to try to avoid a fight. There was a considerable amount of other evidence pointing to self-defence which was available from the beginning and which could have been pursued. Why did Mr Silcott's lawyers put forward a defence which didn't correspond to the evidence, starting with the first statement ("proof of evidence") made by their client?

The person who had most to do with the legal defence was Stephen Christopher, an unqualified legal clerk. Mr Silcott had no previous experience of Mr Christopher as a lawyer, nor had he used his firm before. But Mr Christopher was also a Black man who was known in the Broadwater Farm community and was a friend of the Jarrett family, including Floyd Jarrett, a co-founder of the Youth Association, and his mother, Cynthia Jarrett, whose death was at the centre of the Broadwater Farm events. Not unreasonably, Mr Silcott felt that Mr Christopher was more likely to have his interest at heart, and to understand his predicament. For example, in 1987 Mr Christopher refused to go to Broadwater Farm without a white companion because he was afraid to *"run the gauntlet of the police"*.

There is evidence that Stephen Christopher's boss, solicitor Robert Layton, and barrister Nemone Lethbridge and her pupil Jean Kerr, all knew that the defence they were putting forward was untrue and that it contradicted the evidence on the circumstances of Mr Smith's death.

Mr Silcott, after suffering years of police harassment, had every reason to trust his legal adviser above the police. It was the lawyers' job to represent him according to the facts of the case. Instead they suppressed evidence, turned down witnesses who corroborated their client's initial instructions, and advised him to lie at the trial. They could now come forward and take responsibility for their negligence and mistakes. So far they have chosen to change their story, denying any knowledge of what they obviously knew. The solicitors "lost" the two crucial documents which prove Mr Silcott's case: the "proof of evidence", Mr Silcott's original statement; and a statement made by a police officer DS Hill who was told by a witness that Smith started the fight. Barrister Nemone Lethbridge denies knowing about the "proof of evidence" even though Jean Kerr refers to it in a note to her.

The lawyers are guilty of illegal, unprofessional and unethical conduct. Yet it is Winston Silcott who is being punished for this, not the lawyers.

Not an 'ordinary' conviction

Once Winston Silcott had been arrested and charged with the murder of PC Blakelock, the Smith trial took on another significance for the police. Their falsification of evidence in the Blakelock case indicates how much they wanted the murder of Keith Blakelock to be pinned on Silcott "the troublemaker".

The murder conviction for Smith helped ensure that the Blakelock trial was prejudiced from the start. As with Paul

34

Hill, a victim of the Guildford Four miscarriage of justice, Mr Silcott's conviction in one case helped to convict him in another. Also like Paul Hill, Mr Silcott was discouraged from taking the witness stand in the Blakelock case because he already had a murder conviction (for Anthony Smith). Therefore he was unable to deny in his own words the lies his accusers put forward during his trial. This must have contributed to the guilty verdict: evidence shows that defendants who don't take the stand are more likely to be convicted.

Not only was the Blakelock trial influenced by the Smith case; the Smith trial itself was influenced by the Blakelock case. As soon as Silcott was charged for Blakelock two things happened. Winston Silcott was now in prison not for Smith but for Blakelock. The murder charge for Anthony Smith seemed of lesser importance compared to the enormity of having been falsely accused of killing a police officer. Secondly, according to Mr Silcott, the legal team that was working on the Smith case, and Winston himself, switched their attention to the Blakelock murder charge and started working on that, to the neglect of the Smith case.

If the Blakelock case overshadowed the Smith case for the Silcott defence team, the Smith case took on a greater significance for the police. Before the Smith trial Mr Silcott's name was in the papers in relation to Blakelock. Even if none of the jurors had seen this, they would have known that Winston Silcott the accused lived in Broadwater Farm which had been described as a "jungle" and whose Black residents had been called "hyenas", etc., in the tabloids. They would have put this together with the fact that during the Smith trial they were escorted into the court by police (a treatment usually reserved for "terrorists" or mass murderers), and that police officers (from the Blakelock investigation) packed the court room. All this would have affected the jury.

At the end of the Smith trial the judge mentioned that Winston Silcott was on remand for the murder of PC Blakelock. The Home Secretary set his tariff (the minimum he has to serve) at 14 years — higher than average for a "murder" which happened during a fight which the accused did not start and in which both men were armed with knives.

When the Court of Appeal quashed the Blakelock conviction there was an expectation among people familiar with the case that the Smith conviction would be referred back to the Appeal Court. Instead whenever Mr Silcott's case has been assessed, inconsistencies among witnesses about details which are not substantive have been used to dismiss their entire statements. Yet all the witnesses agree on the substantive question that Winston Silcott acted to protect himself from Smith's attack. The legal Establishment's refusal to refer the case back to the Appeal Court seems to have more to do with the political climate surrounding the Blakelock case than with the evidence in the Smith case.

As *Climate of Fear* concluded in 1992:

". . . 'justice requires' that the Smith case be reopened."
(p.246)

". . . the Home Office seems bent on exacting retribution, not reconsidering Silcott's conviction." (p.245)

Mr Silcott has already served 12 years in prison. There is no guarantee that he will be released after 14 years. Prisoners protesting their innocence are usually refused parole because they do not "show remorse". How do you "show remorse" for a crime you haven't committed!

Given that Winston Silcott has already been the victim of one high profile miscarriage of justice, it can reasonably be expected that the criminal justice system would take particular care to ensure that his second conviction is safe. But instead of reviewing all the evidence in public view so that justice can be seen to be done, one false conviction is being used to reinforce the other.

The influence of a police/media witch-hunt

Since the Blakelock conviction was overturned, there have been repeated attempts by the Police Federation, the political arm of the police, to determine the course of justice. It is widely believed that Mr Silcott's case has not been reviewed because the police are actively opposing a review which might get him out of prison.

> *"Police officers have told me explicitly that as long as he remains in jail, the blow to morale caused by the quashing of the Blakelock convictions remains endurable."* (*Climate of Fear* p.246)

The police and media together have tried to prevent Mr Silcott from getting legal aid in his action for damages for his quashed conviction. They have campaigned to get his compensation award withdrawn. In July 1997, Police Federation chairman, Mike Bennett, objected to a reception in honour of Mr Silcott's mother and father which Black Women for Wages for Housework held jointly with us: *"Why is it certain members of the black community only want to help criminals — and murderers to boot?"* The police have continued to comment publicly as if Mr Silcott is guilty of PC Blakelock's murder. None of this is acceptable — the police are in charge of law enforcement, not the courts or the Home Office. Yet hardly anyone in the legal establishment or the media which has reported Police Federation comments has voiced objections to their ignoring or contradicting legal judgments and in this way interfering with a person's ability to get justice. Almost unanimously the media backed the police, adding their own wildly racist comments. They have called him an *"animal"*, a *"killer ape"*, a *"savage"*, accused him of *"voodoo"*, etc.

Sir David Calcutt, who awarded compensation to Winston Silcott after the conviction for the murder of PC Blakelock was quashed, commented about the media's *"comprehensive destruction of Mr Silcott's and his family's name in the national consciousness"*. (See chronology, 4 August 1994.) While evidence offered in Winston Silcott's defence is treated with scepticism and disdain, the police and the media have been allowed to say whatever they like against Mr Silcott. We are a multi-racial women's group which has had to confront violent men and help women take a private prosecution against a rapist. We take great exception to Scotland Yard's implication that Winston Silcott, who has neither record nor reputation for attacking women, is a rapist who should stay in jail for our protection. Why are the police trying to impose this dangerous racist stereotype on him and on the public? And why don't they *"care if he's guilty or not"*?

This witch-hunt, in part because those in authority have never shown disapproval, has been found acceptable in many legal circles; that is, it has been taken as a true and accurate reading of events and personalities. This background presents a grave danger to anyone trying, after all these prejudiced years, to be objective.

The onus is now on the criminal justice system to show that its process of assessment and its decisions in the Smith case are not tainted by the torrent of racist lies and slanders which it has allowed police and media to cast against this one man. It is our hope that the chronology which follows, which aims to free the account of the Silcott case of stereotypes, slanders and racist malice, will help finally to clear the Silcott name.

Nina Lopez-Jones

Chronology of injustice

1980

Winston Silcott, who lives on Broadwater Farm Estate in Tottenham, London, is tried and acquitted for the murder of Lennie McIntosh. The facts of the case show that he should not even have been prosecuted but the police have continued to refer to this case as if Silcott had been found guilty.

1981

Dolly Kiffin and a number of young people from Broadwater Farm including Silcott, Floyd Jarrett, Delroy Lindo and Stafford Scott, form the Broadwater Farm Youth Association.

1983

Silcott owns and runs a greengrocer shop on the estate. Although he has convictions for burglary and one for malicious wounding he does not have the reputation for violence which the police and the media have given him. On the contrary. He is respected on the estate as a community spokesperson and as someone who tries to deflate and prevent conflicts and violence. Silcott regularly attends meetings of Haringey Council's Police Sub Committee. The Committee is made up of councillors and over 30 non-voting delegate groups representing Black and ethnic minority groups, women's groups, young people, older people and lesbian and gay people.

Sir Kenneth Newman, Commissioner of the Metropolitan Police labels inner-city multi-racial neighbourhoods as "symbolic locations" specifically mentioning four areas of London: Railton

Road in Brixton, All Saints Road in Notting Hill, Finsbury Park, and Broadwater Farm. In a speech to the right-wing European Atlantic Group he says *"There are two particular problems in the Western societies which have the potential to effect the balance between order and freedom. The first problem is concerned with the growth of multi-ethnic communities. The second is related to indigenous terrorist movements engaging in terrorism to promote separatism or an extreme ideology."*

1984

A serious ongoing dispute develops between Anthony Smith, a professional boxer who has a record for violence, and his friends Wayne Jones and Renton Nelson who call themselves the Yankees, and Mark Nash who is a friend of George Silcott, Winston's younger brother. The Yankees have a reputation in the community for violence and boast that they carry guns. Jones and Nelson also have convictions for violence.

The dispute escalates when Nash takes some goods from Smith in lieu of money Smith owes him. Nash says in a statement submitted as part of Silcott's appeal: *"Shortly after this, Jones, Smith and two others came to my home. Outside my home I was threatened with a gun."* On another occasion *"Smith and Jones confronted me outside the greengrocers shop run by Winston Silcott . . . Winston Silcott came out of the shop and other people came out from the nearby Youth Association."* This prevented the attack.

On one other occasion Nash is being chased by the Yankees *"with open knives. I ran into the party and into an upstairs room where Winston Silcott was running a bar. Smith and the others came in and threatened to kill me. However, because of the presence of Silcott and other people from the Broadwater Farm they did not assault me and they left."* The next day Smith, Jones and Nelson follow Nash to the Youth Association premises. *"Jones put a bag down on the bar and took out a double-barrelled shotgun. Smith pulled out a very large knife and came for me."* People at the Youth Association say that the dispute is getting out of hand and that it should be settled by a fist fight outside. This happens in front of a crowd of people and Nash wins. However, Smith does not let the matter drop. Three or four weeks later Nash is walking in Wood Green when *"Smith came up behind me and slashed me across the throat with a large knife."* Nash shows Silcott the cut later that day and Silcott advises him to go home and keep out of sight.

The violent dispute between Smith and his gang, and Mark Nash, including the incident where Jones came to the Youth Association premises with the shotgun, is confirmed in statements by four witnesses. The statement by Dolly Kiffin, chair of the Youth Association, about the incident with the shotgun also says: *"I asked the Police to come straight away. The Police never came."* According to Mary Silcott, Silcott's mother, although the police were in and out of Broadwater Farm they weren't likely to come when residents called them. This is confirmed by many witnesses who later give evidence to the Broadwater Farm Inquiry chaired by Lord Gifford (see "Not an 'ordinary' conviction" above).

One witness to this shotgun incident at the Youth Association also reports that Jones threatened to *"shoot"* Silcott. Several people give statements in a similar vein. For example, Michael Scott says that during the months before Smith's death it became *"common knowledge around North London after the incident that Smith and the others had been going around threatening to kill Silcott. I remember speaking to Silcott about a week after the incident which I have described and warning him."*

15 December

Winston Silcott is attacked with a knife by Anthony Smith at a party in Hackney. Silcott tries to avoid a fight and pushes Smith away. He then feels a cut on his face, lashes out in self-defence and stabs Smith. Smith is pulled away by his friends Jones and Nelson and leaves, still swearing and shouting at Silcott. No-one seems to think that the wounds will prove fatal since Smith walks away. When Jones and Nelson take Smith to hospital they are questioned by police and refuse to give their names or any information. They are arrested for attempted murder and subsequently released.

A week later Smith dies in hospital.

1985

4 February

Judith Young, a 17-year-old who was at the party, gives a statement to the police. *"A man came from the area between the sound system and the far wall. He deliberately bashed into Sticks [Silcott's nickname] . . . I got the impression that the smaller man [Smith] had drawn a knife but I didn't see it . . . A fight started[;] Sticks cut the other man's head and face and punched him in his stomach or chest. I didn't see a knife in his hand but he has a big hand and I couldn't see from the angle I was standing . . . I should mention that when the [fight] began Sticks was pushing the other man away. He didn't appear to want to fight . . . It finished when the smaller guys friends two of them came from behind the other man [Smith], from the same direction he had come. They led the injured man away out of the room. The injured man shouted and swore at Sticks when he was taken out . . . I noticed that police were outside. I mentioned it to Sticks but he appeared unconcerned."*

13 February

Silcott hears that the police are looking for him in connection with the stabbing of Smith. He goes to solicitors Antony Steel & Co. and makes a statement saying that he acted in self-defence. He explains: *". . . I attended at my Solicitors' office on 13 February 1985. On that occasion, I gave a truthful account of the incident to a Solicitor's representative. . . . He repeated what I told him into a dictaphone. My recollection is that he also took notes."* Silcott is not given a copy of his own statement — as is common. The solicitors later say that this statement is lost (see 7 April 1987).

Silcott agrees to meet his solicitor and to go with him to the police station.

16 February

When Silcott again goes to the solicitors' the police are waiting for him. He is arrested, kept in for two days and questioned. *"On the same day or the day after I was arrested at my Solicitors' office. The following day I was interviewed by the Police in the presence of Stephen Christopher [the solicitors' clerk]. At the time of the interviews, I did not know what evidence the Police had against me and I thought the best course was to deny all knowledge of the incident which I did."*

Silcott's refusal to volunteer information at the police station is not surprising since this is the advice of his solicitor. Somebody who is being questioned at the police station would not ignore his solicitor's advice, especially if, as with Silcott, he has no reason to think that if he tells the truth the police will believe him.

Silcott is charged with the murder of Anthony Smith. He is refused bail and kept in prison on remand.

From this point Stephen Christopher, an unqualified legal clerk, is, as Silcott says, *"the person who had the greatest part to play in the preparation of my defence"*. This is confirmed by a reported conversation with Robert Layton, the solicitor supervising Christopher. For the case of a client facing a murder charge for which he could get life, to be prepared by an unqualified legal clerk seems grossly negligent of the solicitors, and would seem enough by itself to justify an appeal.

25 February

Christopher visits his client in prison and tells him that no-one can confirm he killed Smith. Silcott explains in a later statement that *"He [Christopher] told me that, if the prosecution were unable to prove that I had used a knife, it would be extremely unwise of me to admit that I had stabbed Smith. . . . I was deeply concerned at my predicament. I trusted Stephen Christopher as my legal adviser and felt that he knew best how to conduct my defence."* Silcott, on Christopher's legal advice, agrees to say that *"I had been given a knife by another man during the fight but I had never actually used it."*

During this period Christopher interviews a number of eyewitnesses who confirm that Smith provoked the fight and that Silcott acted to save his own life. None of these witnesses is pursued by Christopher. The only statement taken by Christopher is from Christopher's friend Michael Jarrett, who says that Silcott acted in self-defence but did not have a knife. However, in a later statement (14 June 1995) Jarrett admits to Andrew Hall, Silcott's solicitor at that time, that Silcott did have a knife.

4 March

A letter from Antony Steel & Co. to the clerk of Nemone Lethbridge, the barrister employed to represent Silcott, refers to a "detailed statement" by Silcott. Instructions to Nemone Lethbridge shortly after say, *"... Counsel [barrister] will see the Defendant has supplied I.S. [instructing solicitor, Antony Steel] with **a very detailed statement** to give counsel a picture of the offence for which he is charged."* Silcott says this is the first statement he gave to his solicitors where he describes how Smith attacks him and he defends himself. This is the statement which Antony Steel later says is lost (see 7 April 1987).

28 May

Committal hearing for the murder of Anthony Smith. Silcott pleads not guilty. Judith Young gives evidence but denies seeing anything. She has previously told the police that Smith provoked the fight and seemed to have a knife.

31 May

Silcott is released on bail because the evidence that Silcott stabbed Smith, which Silcott is denying, is considered by the judge to be weak.

28 September

In Brixton, Cherry Groce is shot in her bed during a night raid on her home by police looking for her son. As a result she has a permanent disability which confines her to a wheelchair. The community takes to the streets in protest. Commander Marnoch announces that the officer who shot Mrs Groce will be suspended while an inquiry into the shooting is carried out.

5 October

Floyd Jarrett, a founder of the Broadwater Farm Youth Association, is arrested. Whilst he is being held Detective Constable Randall comes into the police station. Randall has been moved from Stoke Newington police station and already in the summer of 1985 two complaints have been made against him for his conduct during house searches. Though off duty, he orders a search of Jarrett's house. He then goes on the search with other officers. Randall takes Jarrett's keys from Jarrett's possessions and uses them to let the police into the house, bursting in without knocking and without producing a search warrant. (All this is illegal.) During the search Randall pushes Jarrett's mother, who has a heart attack and collapses. Whilst her daughter is calling an ambulance the officers continue to search the house. Mrs. Jarrett dies before the ambulance arrives.

6 October

People on the estate are shocked and angry at Mrs. Jarrett's death and demand that the police officers involved in the search be suspended whilst the incident is investigated (as the police had done when Mrs Groce was shot in Brixton). Deputy Assistant Commissioner Richards refuses. The police prevent people from marching to Tottenham police station to protest by blocking all exits to the estate — a kind of mass house arrest. A major conflict erupts on Broadwater Farm which results in the death of Police Constable Keith Blakelock.

7-9 October

An Asian man describes the attitude of reporters who spoke to him on 7 October: *"When the newspapers interviewed me the next day, they wanted me to say it was black against white. When I said it wasn't, they didn't really want to know anything. It didn't make headlines."* (Broadwater Farm Inquiry)

Instead the press reports:

8 October *"A daily war being. waged against white families by younger members of a burgeoning black community who occupy virtually all the flats in the 12 blocks of grey, stained concrete which make up the divided zone."* (*Daily Mail*)

9 October *"The local name for the 12 blocks of flats is Alcatraz, and if you are poor and white, old and ill, it is a vicious and frightening prison. White people there feel they are living in an alien and terrrifying land and nobody will even listen to them, let alone help them."* (*Daily Mail*) Such racist reporting is reinforced by headlines about "hyenas", "butchers" and "monsters".

Cliff Ford, estate sweeper and active Tenants Association member, tells the Broadwater Farm Inquiry: *"I wrote to the Daily Mail myself and said, 'what about the Christmas dinners, the social things the Youth Association does?' They didn't want to know about that, they never published that at all."*

Although 25% of those later arrested for rioting, affray, etc., are white, the police and media hide white people's involvement in the conflict or dismiss them as "outside agitators".

The press targets Councillor Bernie Grant after his comments: *"I find it difficult to condemn anyone for what happened after the death of an innocent woman."* and *"The reason Sir Kenneth Newman is threatening the use of rubber bullets is because on Sunday night the police got a bloody good hiding . . ."*

Under the headline *"DON'T CALL ME BARMY BERNIE"* the *Sun* describes Councillor Grant as *"peeling a banana and juggling an orange"* and claims to quote an unnamed Labour councillor as saying: *"Bernie Grant is like the leader of a black tribe — always looking for battles and shaking his spear. He sees all whites as his enemy."*

11 October

Detective Sergeant Hill makes a statement reporting a conversation he had with Terry Hoffman, a doorman at the party where Smith was stabbed. Hoffman, he says, told him, ***"You know between you and me the dead guy caused it all. . . . He came*** *in with a knife cut Sticks and Sticks defended himself."* This confirms what Silcott has said: that when Smith attacked him he felt a nick on his face and afterwards saw that he had been cut across the nose by Smith. He still has a scar. Hoffman tells DS Hill that Smith was *"Definitely a nutter"* and that *"Everybody thought the guy [Smith] was coming back so I told Sticks to clear off."* Hoffman later makes a statement to this effect (see 17 September 1992). **DS Hill's statement is available to the defence lawyers before the trial but is never pursued by them.** Hoffman's statement to Hill clearly indicates that Silcott acted in self-defence.

There is another record of a conversation between Hoffman and DS Hill of which DS Hill takes notes. Hoffman is not asked to sign a statement, he is asked to come back to the police station the next day which he does. Hoffman confirms he doesn't want to make a statement but says he will go to court if the police want him to.

DS Hill dies in 1987.

12 October

Silcott is arrested in connection with the death of PC Blakelock. He is denied access to a solicitor, held incommunicado and interviewed on five occasions over a period of two days. He is then charged with the murder of PC Blakelock.

14 October

Winston Silcott is named in numerous front page articles and news bulletins.

"ACCUSED . . . Silcot [sic], 26, a greengrocer, of Martlesham, Broadwater Farm Estate, Tottenham, was taken under armed escort to Paddington Green police station, which is normally reserved for terrorists and other 'highly dangerous' prisoners. The police station, which has a network of underground cells, was chosen because it was feared that his arrest could spark further violent demonstrations. Silcott's 21-year-old brother, who was arrested separately, was being questioned at a North London police station." (front page, *Daily Mail*)

"TWO MORE ON PC MURDER CHARGE . . . A man and a 14-year-old youth were charged last night with the murder of PC Keith Blakelock . . . Winston Emmanuel Silcott, whose brother is being questioned in connection with the killing, was arrested when he reported to a North London police station where armed officers were waiting." (Daily Mail)

"THREE ON PC DEATH CHARGE . . . Two more people were charged last night with the murder of PC Keith Blakelock . . . The second youth and Winston Emmanuel Silcott, a greengrocer from Martlesham, Broadwater Farm Estate, Tottenham, are to appear at Tottenham Magistrates Court today." (front page, Daily Telegraph)

15 October

"A boy of 14 and a 28-year-old greengrocer were yesterday charged with the murder of PC Keith Blakelock during the riots in Tottenham, London . . . Magistrates had to tell black shop-keeper Winston Silcott to 'pay attention' while the charge was read . . . Silcott, of Broadwater Farm Estate, had only socks on his feet and was wearing a striped prison shirt." (Sun)

"TWO FACE RIOT MURDER COURT . . . A greengrocer age 26 and a 14-year-old boy were yesterday remanded in custody charged with the murder of Police Constable Keith Blakelock in the riots eight days ago . . . Winston Emmanuel Silcott, of the Broadwater Farm Estate, was remanded for seven days at Tottenham . . . Both defendants are black." (Daily Express)

"Winston Silcott, a black greengrocer, and a 14-year-old black youth were remanded in custody yesterday charged with the murder of PC Keith Blakelock during the Tottenham rioting on October 6. Silcott of Martlesham, Broadwater Farm, chatted to relatives in the gallery at Tottenham magistrates court while the charge was read. Magistrate Mr Samuel Kershwen agreed to a plea by Det Insp Max Dingle that the hearing be moved to a more secure court." (Daily Telegraph)

The police investigating Blakelock's death act illegally and ignore legal rights: heavy-handed arrests including breaking

48

down the doors of 18 homes on the estate, holding people in police stations for long periods, denying them access to solicitors and the right to inform relatives and friends of where they are and lengthy interrogations. Gabriel Black, a local solicitor who defended over 20 people arrested at the time said: *"We were told repeatedly that this case was so overwhelmingly serious we would have to bite our tongues and accept whatever the police did. It was absolutely unique in my experience."* (quoted in *A Climate of Fear: The Murder of PC Blakelock and the Case of the Tottenham Three*, David Rose, Bloomsbury 1992)

November/December

The same legal team which has been preparing Silcott's defence in the Smith case now turns its attention to the Blakelock case. It is clear that the Smith case is neglected as a result.

Christopher visits Silcott and tells him that the one prosecution witness in the Smith case who told the police that Silcott had a knife gave a different story at the committal hearing. Therefore Silcott should now *"deny any possession of a knife"*. Faced with a second murder charge, this time for killing a police officer, which has caused a huge police and media outcry, Silcott agrees. From the time Silcott was arrested for Blakelock it took three months for the police to produce any evidence to support that charge. During that time rumours are rife in prison about what the police will do to get evidence to pin Blakelock's murder on Silcott. After the three months the only evidence the police are able to produce is one statement of 26 words — the very statement which years later the ESDA test will prove to be false (see 25 November 1991).

Mary Silcott says that during this period the family received *"endless disgusting, racist letters and anonymous phone calls"*. Some calls during the night threaten: *"You are next."* Rubbish and dog faeces are put through their door. When they report the incidents to the police they are laughed at. The police are themselves involved in persecuting Silcott's family. George, Winston Silcott's younger brother, is constantly picked up by the police, insulted, threatened and accused of all kinds of crimes. On one occasion George Silcott was arrested for rape and made to take part in an identity parade. George Silcott heard later that the woman had already identified her attacker before George was arrested. (All this is illegal.) The family is eventually forced to move from Broadwater Farm and is rehoused by the council.

1986

The Smith trial

28 January

The Recorder of the court makes an order for police protection for jury and witnesses in the forthcoming Smith trial. Protection from what, one must ask. This procedure, normally reserved for trials of those who are considered "terrorists", can only give the entirely false impression to the jury and the media that the police consider Silcott to be a very dangerous man who is part of a network of armed people. The grounds for the court allowing this procedure, which could not but bias the jury, have never been publicly spelled out. Nor has it been officially questioned or criticised in any way. Silcott's barristers do not oppose the protection order. Why not?

3 February

After four months in prison on remand for the murder of PC Blakelock, Silcott goes to trial for the murder of Anthony Smith. There are police gunmen on the roof as Silcott is taken to court.

Many senior police officers attend the trial; they include not only those involved in the Smith case but also those in the Blakelock case such as Detective Chief Superintendent Melvin and Detective Inspector Dingle who will both later be tried for fabricating evidence against Silcott in the Blakelock case. The extraordinary attention the police pay to the Smith trial begins to indicate how connected the two cases were for them. Members of the public in court report that when Silcott is convicted there is a "football match atmosphere" among police officers who stand and cheer and congratulate each other.

Members of the jury in the Smith case are bound to have seen the front page press coverage announcing Silcott's arrest for the Blakelock murder. They would have seen the widespread attacks by the press on the Black residents of Broadwater Farm in the aftermath of the events of 5 October describing them as "hyenas", etc. They obviously know that Silcott lives on Broadwater Farm and therefore it would be astonishing if none of the 12 jurors realise that the man they are trying for Smith's death — and against whom they are getting police protection — is the man accused of Blakelock 's murder. **This likelihood and possible prejudicial effects on the Smith jury is never raised in court.**

The prosecution

Judith Young gives evidence that Smith started the fight by bashing into Silcott — *"He [Smith] had two friends who were trying to drag him away . . ."* — and that he shouted and swore at Silcott as he was being taken out after the stabbing. Young is the key witness; her version of events remains consistent from her statement to the police on 4 February 1985, through the trial and in all statements since.

Roxanne Walden who gave a statement to the police on 1 February 1985 saying that she saw Smith holding a knife, retracts her statement in court. She is treated as a hostile witness and cross-examined about her statement but she denies knowing anything.

Wayne Jones and ***Renton Nelson*** give evidence to say they were in the doorway of the room when the fight happened and did not see the fight. They say that Silcott follows them out shouting and waving a knife. This is denied by Silcott and other witnesses. The trial transcript shows that Jones admits he drew a knife. Jones also says that the three of them had been to other parties and had been drinking. He says he had drunk five glasses of rum.

The defence

Winston Silcott is represented by barristers Robert Harman QC and Nemone Lethbridge. The lawyers put forward the defence that Silcott fought with Smith but did not stab him. They do not address the fact that Smith died of stab wounds and that no-one other than Silcott was seen fighting with him. Silcott is the only witness to appear in his defence. Following his then lawyers' advice, he denies having a knife. He also says that he just pushed Smith away and that he saw Smith's two friends *"outside the door. . . They had knives in their hands."* No evidence is presented that Silcott acted in self-defence or even that Smith had ·threatened to kill him.

In order to make their untruthful defence, the lawyers have had to suppress all evidence of the truth, denying Silcott witnesses and explanations which could have led to his acquittal.

If the prosecution evidence provided by Judith Young and other witnesses had been put in the context of Smith's history of death threats of which the defence was aware, it would have been clear that Silcott acted in self-defence.

One witness, _Dalton Mitchell,_ turns up in court during the trial and offers to give evidence that Silcott acted in self-defence. He is told by Christopher that he will not be called. His statement of 24 November 1987 (below) says: *"When he was pushed backwards by Winston Silcott, Smith's arm was in the air and I clearly saw a blade. During the fight I saw Tony [Wayne] Jones coming towards the two men with a knife in his hand . . . After Winston Silcott's arrest, I saw Stephen Christopher on a number of occasions . . . It was obvious from our conversations that he knew about the conflict between Smith and Nash. It was also obvious to me from what he said that he knew that Winston Silcott had a knife and that he stabbed Smith . . . "*

A number of statements which point to self-defence are not pursued for the trial: a statement by **_DS Hill_** reporting a conversation with **_Terry Hoffman_** the doorman, where Hoffman con-

52

firms *"the dead guy caused it all. He came in with a knife cut Sticks and Sticks defended himself."* **_Vibert Nelson_** saying he heard people say that Silcott was cut first. **_Erskine Braithwaite_** saying he heard that Smith pulled out a penknife and cut Silcott. **_Mark Nash_** on the conflict between Smith's gang on the one hand, and himself and Silcott on the other.

Every witness to the killing confirms that Smith started the fight by "bashing" into Silcott and that Silcott tried to avoid a fight and tried to push Smith away.

All this evidence clearly pointed to self-defence. The defence could and should have pursued all or any part of it. Much later Adrian Clarke, Silcott's present solicitor, will find Terry Hoffman and ask him to make a statement. Christopher or Layton should have done this. They didn't.

This all points clearly to the fact that Christopher told Silcott to lie and actively suppressed any evidence of self-defence. If Silcott had wanted to deceive his lawyers, why would he have made the first truthful statement on 13 February 1985, and why would he have continued to tell people, such as Dalton Mitchell, that he was going to plead self-defence? Both the solicitor and the junior barrister, both of whom had all the papers, must have known that the defence put forward in court was not the truth.

Although none of the witnesses who give evidence in court say that they saw a knife in Smith's hand, neither do they see a knife in Silcott's hand. But everyone agrees that both Smith and Silcott must have had knives. In fact, a police search at the hospital confirms that **Smith, Jones and Renton were all armed with knives**. At the hospital knives are taken by police from Smith's clothes and also from Jones and Nelson. Wayne Jones admits in court he was carrying a knife and drew it at one point.

The knives of Smith, Jones and Nelson when tested are shown to have blood on them. Scientists at the time are unable to say whether the blood on Smith's knife is Silcott's — DNA tests were less sophisticated then — only that "the possible presence of blood had been obtained."

7 February

The jury convicts Silcott for the murder of Anthony Smith and he is sentenced to life imprisonment. In sentencing, the judge acknowledges that *"the stabbing occurred on the spur of the moment . . ."* Prior to sentencing the prosecution asks whether Silcott was *"returned to custody in October, **having been charged with the murder of Police Constable Blakelock . . ?"*** The defence barrister objects that *"the circumstances of his arrest last October have nothing whatever to do with the circumstances which your Lordship has to sentence him for at this stage."*

29 May

Winston Silcott changes solicitors from Antony Steel & Co. to Hodge, Jones and Allen (HJA). Silcott tells Andrew Hall of HJA that he acted in self-defence and Hall starts to trace witnesses and gather new evidence to support this.

Hall spends 10 months trying to get the papers transferred from Antony Steel & Co. When the papers arrive, Silcott's original statement and DS Hill's statement — the most crucial evidence to prove self-defence — are missing (see 7 April 1987).

However, Hall does find in the papers notes made by trainee barrister Jean Kerr, Nemone Lethbridge's pupil. The notes are undated but had to have been written before Robert Harman QC is instructed, three weeks before the trial begins, in February 1986. The notes are headed *"Nemone herewith (please) my contributions re: Silcott."*

The notes refer in detail to *"Sticks' own statement — he tells how . . . another man offered him a knife so that he could protect himself . . ."* The statement to which this note refers can only be Silcott's first statement to Antony Steel & Co. on 13 February 1985. It is this statement which is later "lost". Kerr's notes also refer in detail to the history of conflict between Smith, Jones and Nelson, and Nash.

16 September

Christopher makes a statement to Silcott's solicitor Andrew Hall which refers to Silcott's original statement: *"I do not know the date that the original proof of evidence was taken . . .",* again confirming that there was a statement. Christopher also says that they explored the dispute between Smith and Nash as well as the issue of self-defence. He also says that he tried to delay the court date but the barristers thought the case was ready to go to trial. *"I was very unhappy that the case was going ahead because I did not think that it was ready for trial."* Considering he had nearly a year to prepare the case, this is shocking. **This again raises the issue of negligence by defence lawyers.** Can it be that Christopher at first thought the evidence against Silcott was weak and so Silcott should deny everything; but that once Silcott was charged for Blakelock, Christopher realised that the police would be determined to get Judith Young to give evidence, and therefore that the line of defence which he had told Silcott to follow could not work? Silcott paid the price for this illegal manipulation of the evidence. Lethbridge confirms that Christopher wanted the trial postponed when interviewed by Andrew Hall (11 August 1987). Why did the barristers refuse to postpone the trial date?

17 December

Robert Layton, the solicitor supervising trainee Christopher, is interviewed by Andrew Hall. *Layton avoids making a formal statement at this time or later.* In a letter to Antony Steel, Hall records what Layton said during the interview: *"Mr Layton saw our client at an early stage of the proceedings and recalls taking a proof of evidence from him which he, Mr Layton, would have dictated onto a machine. Thereafter the conduct of the case was in the hands of Mr Christopher throughout, although Mr Layton recalls assisting from time to time . . . Mr Layton does not recall the content of the original instructions taken and is unable to say, one way or the other, whether Mr Silcott originally said that he was in possession of a knife at the relevant time. In retrospect, Mr Layton thought that if he had said this, and then denied it subsequently, Mr Layton would have recollected the earlier conflicting statement. However, Mr Layton could not be absolutely sure on the point. He agreed that, in those circum-*

55

*stances, he would have been professionally embarrassed. Mr Layton was shown a letter dated 4th March 1985 addressed to the Clerk to Miss Lethbridge, of Counsel, from your firm which enclosed statements by Silcott and Mark Nash. He was also shown a copy of instructions to Counsel in the Old Street Magistrates Court which stated that 'The Defendant has supplied instructing solicitors with a very detailed statement to give Counsel a picture of the offence for which he is charged.' **Mr Layton agreed that these documents indicated that, at an early stage, a full proof of evidence had been obtained from the client."***

Andrew Hall tries at least three times to get a written statement from Layton but Layton cancels. Hall asks the Criminal Appeals Office to contact Layton but Layton never replies.

The Broadwater Farm Inquiry is published. Much of the publicity is favourable but Lord Gifford who chaired the inquiry receives hate mail. *"The likes of you, are Traitors, and have sold us, and our Country, out, to Blacks. You do not believe in Honesty, truth, or FAIR PLAY." "While we have so called people like you in office life is hell when you sympathise with the blacks. This country will never be the same and will get worse thanks to your type." "You dirty cowardly homosexual looking filthy bastard I am getting on a bit but I am going to find out your private address and give you a dam good hiding."*

1987

21 January

The trial for the murder of PC Blakelock begins. The only evidence against Silcott is an unsigned statement of 26 words which he denies making. A statement from 13-year-old Jason Hill, originally one of the defendants, which names Silcott as the ringleader of the group who attacked Blakelock, is ruled inadmissable by the judge, Justice Hodgson, but only after it has been seen by the jury. The judge orders the case against Jason Hill and another teenager to be dismissed. He condemns the police treatment of them.

22 January

On the second day of the trial, *The Sun* publishes the police photograph of Winston Silcott on the front page. This photo was taken just as Silcott woke up; many people have commented that his startled grin makes him look mad and heartless. Its publication with the caption: *"This is the first picture of the man police believe wielded the machete which hacked brave bobby Keith Blakelock to death."* must be considered an attempt to prejudice the jury. Since this is a police photo, only they could have given it to *The Sun*. Is it usual for the police to release photos of people as they go to trial?

23 January

The Sun article is condemned by Justice Hodgson, who says it appears to be a contempt of court and that he will refer it to the attorney-general with a view to possible prosecution. He also criticises the newspaper for publishing a photograph of Silcott. *"This had caused him 'total astonishment' in a case where identification was likely to be an issue: . . . it appears that at least one part of the press cannot be trusted."* (*Guardian*)

10 February

The police determination to get Silcott convicted extends to their bribery and corruption of witnesses. One of the prosecution witnesses, Mr Cobham, *"admitted that he had received police protection, including free accommodation, had been given £40 or £50 by police to buy groceries, and had been 'fixed up' with two jobs by the police."* (*Guardian*)

19 March

Silcott, Mark Braithwaite and Engin Raghip are convicted of the murder of PC Blakelock. By this time Silcott has been on remand for two years.

20 March

After the conviction the media coverage concentrates on vilifying Silcott with a series of inaccurate, false and racist articles which quote the police. They portray Silcott as the ringleader. Although he is not the only one convicted he is the only one targeted in this way: Braithwaite and Raghip are only mentioned. There is little coverage of Justice Hodgson's very severe criticisms of the police investigation and his statements about the lack of evidence against Silcott.

Nearly every article comments that Silcott was on bail for the Smith killing when he was arrested for Blakelock: *"Knifeman who was let loose to murder again."* (*Today*)

Two photos of Silcott are used in all the major newspapers: the police photo with the grin mentioned earlier and another photo also taken at the police station and again released to the press. Silcott says that this second photo is taken when six officers come into the room and grab him. He starts to struggle fearing that he is going to get beaten up. Then the door opens and he sees a photographer with a camera on a tripod positioned just outside the door. As soon as Silcott sees the photographer he puts his arms in front of his face: he is convinced that the police want to take a photo of his face and superimpose it on the body of one of the people photographed on the evening of PC Blakelock's death. But the photo is taken just as the police let go of him and his arms are rising at his side. Many people have commented that this photo attempts to make Silcott look frightening. No-one has condemned the police for behaving — at best — like paparazzi in taking photographs they were not legally or morally entitled to, or for releasing these photos to the media. At the time the photos are taken the police are manufacturing a case against Silcott for a crime he hasn't committed. Can there be any other explanation than that the photos are part of their management of the case to ensure enduring bias?

Press coverage includes (capital letters indicate headlines; bold type is our emphasis):

"One [policeman] said: 'The hold he had on those people was frightening. ***It was like voodoo, the evil eye.'"*** . . . *"He described himself as a greengrocer. But police gave Winston Silcott another title —* ***the Godfather of Broadwater Farm*** *. . . He extorted money as the leading muscleman of the estate's drug*

trade . . . *brave residents, many of them Asians, who tried to stop* **the evil racketeer had their homes fire-bombed."** (*Daily Mirror*)

"THE FACE OF EVIL . . . *This is the man with murder in his eyes and hate in his heart. Winston Silcott led the baying mob which hacked PC Keith Blakelock to death in the Broadwater Farm riots . . . 'The charge was like* **a scene from Zulu.'** *"* (*Today*)

"VICTIM OF THE SAVAGES . . . *Machete monster Winston Silcott was jailed for 30 years yesterday for hacking PC Keith Blakelock to death . . . and he simply smiled . . .* **The giant black gang leader** *. . . Winston Silcott's greengrocery shop — a front for drug-dealing — stood undamaged through the riot. But other stores belonging to* **Asian rivals were wrecked."** (*Sun*)

"AT 12 HE WAS A BULLYING THIEF . . . *Detective Superintendent Graham Melvin, who headed the Blakelock murder investigation said: 'Silcott is a most chilling character. He has absolutely no compunction about using the most extreme violence.'"* (*London Daily News*)

"EVIL SMILE OF HATE . . . *The violent gangster who ruled Broadwater Farm estate with* **a voodoo-like grip of fear** *. . . "* (*Daily Mirror*)

"BLOODY SUNDAY ON BROADWATER FARM . . . *he was also deeply feared partly because he appeared — and believed himself to be — invincible, having been suspected of so many serious offences he was not charged with, and partly because people thought he was capable of knifing anyone who just jogged his arm with a pint in the pub."* (*Daily Mail*)

"30 YEARS FOR BEAST WHO WAS FREED TO KILL AGAIN . . . The monster *who led the gang murder of PC Keith Blakelock* **swaggered from the dock yesterday with a smile on his face . . . it was the FOURTH** [emphasis in original] **time he had been on trial for murder. . .** *They are led by* **an animal called Winston Silcott, who was yesterday caged for life . . .** *For* **he ruled the lawless Broadwater Farm jungle with a reign of terror."** (*Star*)

The headlines hide that the trial is deeply flawed:

"The judge hit out at a catalogue of blunders by police. He condemned their questioning of two of the three teenagers who had murder charges against them dropped during the trial . . . The judge's ruling and comments were made in the absence of the jury and can only be reported now." (Star)

"There was no forensic evidence and no identification evidence from more than 1,000 police photographs presented during the trial. There were no witnesses to give evidence against the accused." (Guardian)

One article spells out the Blakelock-Smith connection:

*"The wall of silence was so strong that the charge of killing Smith was nearly dropped and Silcott was allowed out on bail . . . So police went back over all the witnesses to the Smith murder **determined to nail Silcott for at least one killing.** Finally, a young woman courageously turned up to give evidence at the last minute and Silcott was jailed for life while on remand for killing PC Blakelock."* (Daily Mirror)

While it was only *after* the murder of Blakelock that the police accused Silcott of intimidating witnesses and creating a "wall of silence", this was first used against him in the Smith trial. On sentencing the judge said, *"I have no doubt that at least three of the witnesses who gave evidence for the prosecution were terrified of you."*

In fact as local solicitor, Gabriel Black explains, the police *"frightened the living daylights out of everybody. That's why they were faced with the so-called wall of silence. People were simply terrified."* (Climate of Fear)

The media focusses on Silcott having been on bail at the time of Blakelock's murder. It does not escape everyone that the question of bail for murder suspects distracts from the grave flaws in the Blakelock case. *"There is anxiety that the row over bail for suspected murderers has drawn attention away from the question of the police conduct during their investigations, criticised by the judge, and the feeling that the evidence against at least some of the three was at best flimsy. In Silcott's case it depends almost entirely on a few sentences, open to interpretation, which he uttered in the course of a long series of police interviews . . . Of the 1,000 photographs taken by police during the riot, none shows the distinctive shape or form of Silcott, even though he is said to have been the ringleader. Nor was there any forensic evidence linking him with the riot or the murder."* (Guardian)

The trial judge, Justice Hodgson later says: *"I have never known any trial, before or since, when I felt under such intense pressure."*

7 April

Antony Steel himself writes in response to the investigation by the Criminal Appeals Office in the Smith case to say that *"We believe that a proof of evidence [a statement to the lawyer] was taken at an early stage at or around the time of Mr. Silcott's arrest. This as far as we can recall, was a brief proof . . ."* But a letter from Antony Steel & Co. to Nemone Lethbridge dated 4 March 1985, three weeks after Silcott's arrest, described the same statement as a *"detailed proof"*. This letter from Steel two years later goes on to say *"the earlier proof was misplaced and no copy could be found . . ."* **Silcott says this "proof" would have shown the contradiction between the version of events he related before he got legal advice, and the version he gave on Christopher's advice. In order for this first statement to go missing, three copies had to be lost — the solicitor's, the barrister's and the one for the file.**

11 August

Nemone Lethbridge, the junior barrister in the Smith case, is interviewed by Andrew Hall and says she knows nothing of the history of conflict between Smith and Silcott or that Silcott had a knife.

She says: *"The original proof I had for Mr Silcott was in the very very early days; I was given a proof almost immediately. . . . The first proof . . . just related to his [Silcott's] movements, it didn't relate to his contact with Smith."*

Hall asks her to comment on the notes of her pupil, Jean Kerr (7 February 1985) and Lethbridge says: *"I don't remember what she is referring to that's the difficulty. I had two murder cases at the time that were very similar, both stabbings at Blues parties. Jean Kerr did work on both. I find difficulty in recalling which detail refers to which case. There was a similarity in the two cases and it is difficult in casting one's mind back to remember which was which."* Hall points out that the notes read *"in Sticks own statement . . ."* and therefore must refer to the Smith case and not some other murder trial. Lethbridge admits that *"Well, there must have been a second missing document. . . . I don't remember any of this but then my memory is not that perfect."*

Either, as Kerr's notes indicate, there is an original detailed statement from Silcott, or Lethbridge has conducted Silcott's defence on the basis of a brief statement which only addresses background issues — that is, without any written instructions from her client until three weeks before the Smith trial when the leading barrister Robert Harman is instructed.

Robert Harman says that there was no full "proof of evidence" at the meeting on 14 January 1986. Lethbridge agrees that the "proof" which was used at the trial was prepared after 14 January.

When asked if she knows that *"Smith was part of a gang called The Yankees who used a lot of violence and got themselves into a vendetta to get Nash and Silcott stepped in . . ."* Lethbridge says: *"I knew nothing about that . . ."* If she didn't, why not? Did she not read any of the documents available at the time which refer to this, including her pupil's notes and statements from Wayne Jones, Renton Nelson, DS Hill, Vibert Nelson, Erskine Braithwaite and Mark Nash (3 February 1986)?

She also says: *"I remember that the case was ill-prepared . . . Mr Steele was like the absentee landlord. The Assistant Solicitor Mr Latham and Stephen Christopher came along 90 minutes late . . . then the consultation went short as they were late, not as long as we had hoped . . ."*

13 August

A columnist, Mills of *The Star,* is condemned by the Press Council for *"outrageously racist, crude, offensive and inflammatory"*

remarks. *"The column criticised by the Council headed 'A face to haunt us all' was commenting on the murder of PC Blakelock . . . The columnist said the murderer's* **'dreadful black visage'** *would haunt us for the rest of our lives, adding that the* **'last time he saw anything remotely similar, it was in a cage and eating bananas."** The paper's editor, Lloyd Turner, defends his columnist saying that the Mills column was a *". . . genuine and heartfelt reaction to one of the most violent criminals this country had ever put on trial. Mills was referring to ape-like behaviour. The murderer was gaoled for horrendous crimes, and had behaved very much like* **a wild killer ape."** (*Guardian*)

25 September

Lethbridge's pupil Jean Kerr is interviewed by Andrew Hall, about notes she made for Lethbridge when she was preparing for the trial. Kerr: *"I used to prepare my 'write ups' for Nemone. I would read all the papers and at some point I would write up my impressions."* The notes start **"Note — In Sticks own statement — he tells how somebody else another man offered him a knife so he could protect himself . . ."** Andrew Hall: *"You were obviously looking at the statement of Winston Silcott in which Silcott said he had a knife."* Kerr replies *"Yes it looks like that."* Hall: *"I have shown you two references in your notes. It seems clear you had seen a statement [in] which Silcott says he had a knife and protected himself. There is no doubt about that is there?"* Kerr: **"I agree I wrote that document and that although I can't remember seeing the proof my notes indicate there must have been such a proof and I saw it."** Hall asks Kerr if she *"knew about some earlier altercations between the parties [Smith and Nash]."* She answers *"Yes."*

11 November

Silcott makes a new statement to Andrew Hall explaining that Smith, Jones and Nelson had threatened him on at least three occasions during 1984 and had been overheard by, among others, a taxi driver, boasting that they would kill him before the end of 1984 (Smith's attack on Silcott at the party was on 15 December — very close to the end of that year). Silcott details the background to Smith's attack. He says that Smith made *"threats against Nash and me because they thought I was protecting Nash."*

Silcott says that on the night of the attack he arrived at the party on his own. *"As I went into the party I saw Smith, Jones and Nelson getting out of a car nearby . . . I felt there was going to be trouble and that because they had seen me on my own they would attack me with weapons. I then borrowed a knife from a man I know called Stephen White."* It was not uncommon for people in this circle to carry knives at the time — Smith and his friends had a history in the community of carrying knives and guns. Silcott says that he stopped carrying a knife after he was fined for having one.

He describes the three men coming into the room he is in, not seeing him and starting to leave with Smith last in line. Then Smith sees him and spins round. *"He was a professional boxer and hit me very quickly three or four times in the face. I pushed him backwards. As he went back, I caught a glimpse of something shining in his hand."* The room is dark and Silcott thinks it is a knife. *"I felt a nick on my face and my face was cut."* Silcott says he saw Nelson and Jones armed with knives behind Smith just outside the door. They were prevented from coming in by people rushing out but Silcott was afraid that at any moment Nelson and Jones would be able to get at him. He pulls out the knife he has borrowed from Stephen White and lashes out to defend himself. Smith slumps over and walks out shouting and swearing, helped by his two friends.

Although some people have commented on the number of wounds Silcott inflicted on Smith, they are consistent with the reaction of someone who lashes out in fear of his life. As Silcott later says, *"I didn't mean to kill him. No way. I didn't even know he was dead at first. As the time, I was lashing out in fear. It was a dark room."* (*Guardian*, 25 April 1992)

Silcott explains why he agreed to lie in court: *"Faced with two murder charges, I felt my position was desperate and I agreed to do whatever he [Stephen Christopher] thought best."* Silcott explains his initial reluctance to spell out exactly what

Christopher did: *"While my present solicitors were preparing the PC Blakelock case and considering the present appeal, I was still being visited in prison by Stephen Christopher . . . I was very reluctant to make allegations against him of improper behaviour. Firstly, I did not want to single him out as the instigator of my false defence. He was the only person of Caribbean descent involved in my defence and I felt a certain loyalty in that respect. Secondly, I felt guilty about naming him as the instigator when I believed that he thought he was acting in my best interests."*

Stephen Christopher also had the credibility of being a personal friend of the Jarrett family.

24 November

Andrew Hall takes statements from:

Dalton Mitchell who saw Smith bash into Silcott and says: *"I am certain that Smith had a knife in his hand. When he was pushed backwards by Winston Silcott, Smith's arm was in the air and I clearly saw a blade. During the fight, I saw Tony [Wayne] Jones coming towards the two men with a knife in his hand."*

Mitchell spoke to Silcott after the attack and reports that Silcott said, *"They took me for a target. What am I supposed to do, let them stab me?"* Mitchell goes on : *"When Winston Silcott was on remand in custody I visited him. We did not talk a great deal about the case but **he did say he would be pleading self-defence**. I remember him asking me to contact Mark Nash in order that Nash should make a statement to his Solicitors. I knew that Winston Silcott's solicitor was Stephen Christopher. After Winston Silcott's arrest, I saw Stephen Christopher on a number of occasions . . . It was obvious from our conversations that **he knew about the conflict between Smith and Nash**. It was also obvious to me from what he said that **he knew that Winston Silcott had a knife and that he stabbed Smith . . . I went to the court on, I believe the 2nd day of the trial. I saw Stephen Christopher and asked if I was to give evidence. He told me that they were not going to call me."*

Mark Nash giving the history of the conflict between Smith and himself.

Horace Hardy, **Dolly Kiffin** and **Michael Scott** on incidents they witnessed of the dispute between Smith and Nash including threats to Silcott.

Stephen White saying that Silcott borrowed a knife from him. He says he didn't want to admit this to the police at the time because he was held for 24 hours and thought he was going to be set up for something.

2 December

Kerr gives Andrew Hall nine pages of notes amending the transcript of her interview with him. In these notes she changes her story. She had described Silcott's proof of evidence in her notes to Nemone Lethbridge, she now says: *"I can only say that I think it is most likely that that document was a Statement taken by the Police from Silcott."* But this cannot explain why Kerr's note starts "Note: In Sticks own statement — he tells . . ."; why there is no record anywhere of such a statement; and why no one else has ever mentioned its existence. She goes on: *". . . it is my honest belief that in many (probably most) instances — Miss L[ethbridge] never even saw (the contents of) my Write-Ups."* That is, she denies having said that there was an original statement, and in any case if there was, Lethbridge the barrister would not have seen Kerr's reference to it!

New evidence submitted to the Court of Appeal asking for a full hearing includes statements from **Dalton Mitchell**, **Mark Nash**, **Horace Hardy**, **Dolly Kiffin**, **Michael Scott**, **Stephen White**.

1988

13 December

An application for leave to appeal against the Blakelock convictions is dismissed by Lord Lane, Mr Justice McCowan and Mr Justice Steyn in the Court of Appeal. Lord Lane says there is *"no lurking doubt"* surrounding the conviction. The crucial ESDA evidence has not yet emerged. Immediately after the Blakelock appeal, the appeal for the Smith case **is heard by the same judges** and (not surprisingly) is also rejected. The judges say that where someone puts forward a false defence, *"it will be a very rare case indeed, if ever, in which this Court will consider it necessary or expedient in the interests of justice to allow evidence to be called by a defendant to put forward a new defence. This is most definitely not such a case."*

This would not be the first time that Lord Lane gets it wrong. In 1976 he upheld a husband's right to rape his wife (overturned in 1990). In 1987 he dismissed an appeal by the Birmingham Six saying, *"the longer this case has gone on, the more this court has been convinced the jury was correct."*

1989

George Silcott is stopped by police while driving with a friend. The police accuse him of stealing the car despite the fact that his friend has hire documents. He gives a false name, is taken to police station and is about to be released without charge when the police find out that he is Winston Silcott's brother, at which point, George says: *"Their attitude changed completely"*. He is kept in overnight and charged with a burglary on the other side of town which he denies having anything to do with. George has a prominent scar on the left side of his face. The only evidence comes from witnesses to the burglary who describe seeing the face of the man responsible from the left side yet never mention a scar. George Silcott is convicted and sentenced to 12 months in prison.

Home Secretary sets at 30 years the tariff — recommended minimum time in prison for prisoners sentenced to life imprisonment — Winston Silcott must serve for his murder convictions for Smith and Blakelock.

Silcott is elected honorary president of the London School of Economics (LSE). Leading politicians condemn his election. Students defend the move saying it was their intention to highlight that Silcott did not get a fair trial for Blakelock.

3 May

The police/media open season on Silcott makes him a target for any accusations. During the LSE debate he is accused of being a rapist. The media's sympathy is with his lying accuser. *". . . it was impossible not to sympathise with the lady speaker who made the foul and false accusation that Silcott was also a rapist."* (*Evening Standard*)

1990

12 June

It emerges clearly that the police tortured children to try to get them to incriminate Silcott. Mrs. Barbara Hill, mother of Jason Hill the 13-year-old boy whose charges for the murder of Blakelock were dismissed by the judge, writes to the press in protest against DCS Melvin being cleared of mistreating her son. The Police Complaints Authority had found Melvin guilty but their decision was overturned by the Home Secretary.

She writes *". . . Jason was held in a cell for three days. No-one would give me any information about which police station Jason was being held in . . . I phoned 18 police stations, frantic with worry. Even our solicitor was not able to get access to him, he was held completely isolated from any contact with the outside world . . . I did not have any contact with Jason, or even know where he was until a hearing at Tottenham magistrates court more than 50 hours after his arrest. He was covered in vomit and wrapped in an old blanket . . . All the charges were dropped against Jason . . . By this time he had spent nearly 15 months in custody . . . This episode has ruined my life, Jason's life, all our lives. I have been through a divorce and two heart attacks because of this . . . Det Chief Supt. Melvin is responsible for what happened to us because he was in charge of the investigation . . . If anyone else had done what Mr. Melvin did — keeping a child half naked in a cell like that — they would be in prison today. Why should the police be above the law?"* (*Guardian* Letters)

1991

1 February

A precedent-setting judgment is given in a case very similar to Silcott's. Matthew Richardson lied to his lawyers about what had happened. His lawyers therefore put forward a false defence on his behalf. Mr Justice McCowan, and Lord Lane, **the same judges who had turned down the Silcott appeal on exactly this issue (see 13 December 1988), decide that Richardson's appeal should be allowed because** *"we have to consider whether there is a risk that by reason of his own stupid lies a miscarriage of justice may have occurred."*

March

Adrian Clarke, who has been working with Andrew Hall on the Silcott case, takes over as Silcott's solicitor.

7 November

The Law Society makes an order to investigate Antony Steel & Co., Silcott's first solicitors and the firm for which Stephen Christopher worked.

25 November

Winston Silcott and the other two men convicted for the murder of PC Blakelock are cleared after ESDA tests prove that the police fabricated Silcott's statement on which the whole prosecution was based.

The police announce that a new inquiry into Blakelock's murder is to be set up headed by Commander Perry Nove. The Nove Inquiry grants witness confidentiality and immunity from prosecution. Nine names later emerge of people believed to be responsible for Blakelock's murder — Winston Silcott is not one of them. The names are referred to the Crown Prosecution Service.

Adrian Clarke asks for Smith's knife so that further tests can be done. **He is told by police that the knife was destroyed on 13 September 1989.** This is a serious irregularity since Silcott had lodged an appeal before that date and was contesting his conviction. Further DNA tests could have shown that the blood on Smith's knife was Winston Silcott's.

There is little press coverage of Silcott's sucessful appeal in the Blakelock case, especially compared to the witch-hunt conducted against him when he was convicted. The tabloids concentrate on how Mrs Blakelock feels, an important consideration which should never be used to avoid reporting on the extent of police violence and corruption.

29 November

This acceptance of police illegalities and reluctance to condemn the press coverage of the case are not confined to the tabloids. Melanie Phillips in *The Guardian* defends Melvin who is primarily responsible for the miscarriage of justice which cost three men years of their lives: *"Yet what now are the chances of Mr Melvin getting a fair hearing of his side of this story? He has been condemned in court by no less a person than Roy Amlot QC, who threw in the towel on the basis of Mr Melvin's 'apparent dishonesty'. The Crown Prosecution Service is considering whether Mr Melvin should face criminal charges arising from this case. Yet he has now been condemned in a court with no opportunity to put his own case. Is this natural justice? Or is it rather that in righting one injustice, the system has now perpetrated another?"*

1992

The Home Secretary reconsiders Silcott's tariff now that the Blakelock conviction has been overturned. He reduces it from 30 to 14 years. Adrian Clarke asks for the tariff to be reviewed again on the grounds that the Lord Chief Justice, Lord Lane, has recommended 12 years. The Home Secretary refuses.

23 April

The Solicitors Complaints Bureau further investigates Antony Steel & Co. for alleged breaches of the rules governing solicitors' accounts. Steel & Co. eventually close down.

16 June

Clarke applies to the Home Secretary Michael Howard to have the Smith case referred to the Court of Appeal on the basis of new evidence which includes statements by:

**Terry Hoffman**, doorman at the party, who says he saw a knife in Smith's hand and saw Silcott cut. During an informal conversation at the time of Smith's death, Hoffman told DS Hill that Smith had started the fight (see 11 October 1985). DS Hill's statement only comes to light when Silcott's lawyers apply to the Crown Prosecution Service for the prosecution papers. It is found in the bundle of unused materials they send.

Evidence of a conversation in which Stephen Christopher says that Silcott would never have been convicted of the Smith murder if his original instructions had been maintained and that he feels he let Silcott down by being party to the change.

Silcott's lawyers use the Richardson judgment (1 February 1991) to show that it is not reasonable to refuse to allow Silcott to appeal: _"The additional fact that his legal advisers may have been instrumental in putting forward his 'stupid lies' at trial renders it more necessary and expedient in the interests of justice to receive the evidence."_

The Home Office responds by asking the police to investigate the new points raised by Silcott's lawyers including interviewing witnesses. Given that the police were involved in conducting a vendetta against Silcott, can any investigation they undertake in this case be trusted? And considering massive public evidence of their bias, who will trust them enough to speak frankly to them?

Clarke also addresses the question of how the Blakelock case may have affected Silcott's decision to lie in court in the Smith case: _"The Court in the Smith appeal did not appreciate that, by the time he changed to his trial instructions, Mr Silcott must have been aware that a false confession had been manufactured against him by police officers in the Blakelock case . . . A fresh court reviewing the conduct of his defence might now be more sympathetic to his own readiness to bend the rules at this_ *stressful period in his life particularly if this is being encouraged by Stephen Christopher and condoned by Nemone Lethbridge."*

5 August

Clarke asks the Home Secretary for a decision on the appeal.

17 September

Hoffman makes a statement to the police: *"I saw two men, the taller of the two men [Silcott], was bent over, he had what appeared to be blood on his face or neck. He was holding a flick knife in his right hand. I would say the whole knife was about ten inches in length . . . The smaller man he had a knife also holding it in his right hand . . . I went over to the taller man and asked him if he was alright as I was talking to the taller man, the shorter man left the room . . . The taller man walked past me on the stairs, he said to me he is sorry about the trouble and I advised him to go before the shorter man came back."*

5 October

Detective Superintendent Eric Brown is asked by Detective Inspector Norris of Hackney police who is investigating the points in Terry Hoffman's statement, to make a statement about the original Smith investigation. Brown says that the police had interviewed Hoffman *"on at least four occasions"*, on one occasion for *"in excess of ten hours"*. Brown reports that Hoffman says *"he had seen nothing of the assault . . . we could lock him up as long as we liked, but it would make no difference, he'd seen nothing."* It is Brown's view that Hoffman was *"withholding evidence or not telling the truth. . . . Having been mentioned by a large number of witnesses by name or description, it was obvious that he could not have avoided seeing relevant people or events . . . At no time was there any report that Hoffman had changed his position other than the statement of Detective Sergeant Hill."* The Home Office uses Brown's statement, that Hoffman at the time said he saw nothing, and that he must have seen more than he claimed, to dismiss Hoffman's new statement which finally describes what he *did* see.

Brown also confirms: *"Our knowledge of the disputes between Silcott and members of the Yankees was well known to us through the evidence of Donald Watt who was at that time serving a sentence in Chelmsford Prison. All this evidence was produced to the Director of Public Prosecutions and the Prosecuting Counsel."* But this had not emerged at the trial about Smith's death.

DS Brown later gives evidence for the defence in the trial of Detective Chief Superintendent Melvin and Detective Inspector Dingle, the officers accused of fabricating evidence against Silcott in the Blakelock case.

27 October

Silcott's solicitors meet with the Home Office and get a positive response to the points they raise.

1993

Jason Hill is paid £30,000 compensation from the police for his treatment by Melvin during the investigation in the Blakelock murder.

11 May

The Police Federation, the police officers' trade union, advises Mrs. Blakelock, PC Blakelock's widow, to take private legal action against Silcott to obtain damages. Here again the police maintain Silcott is guilty even after the court has cleared him, and try to use PC Blakelock's widow for this purpose.

1994

January

Clarke threatens to take the Home Secretary to court for delay of the decision about the evidence which they have had for over a year.

31 January

The Home Office finally responds. It refuses to refer the case. Like the Court of Appeal before them the Home Office cites various inconsistencies in the details of different statements as a primary reason for their refusal. This avoids the central issue that all the witnesses confirm that Smith attacked Silcott first.

28 February

Silcott is awarded £17,000 compensation for being wrongfully convicted in the Blakelock case.

July

On the eve of Melvin and Dingle's court case, the Crown Prosecution Service announces that there will be no prosecutions against the nine people named by the Nove Inquiry as responsible for Blakelock's murder. (*In the Name of the Law*, David Rose, Vintage, 1996)

26 July

Detective Chief Superintendent Melvin and Detective Inspector Dingle are cleared of fabricating Silcott's statement. **Though he is the victim of the alleged crime Silcott is never called by the prosecution to give evidence despite making clear that he would be ready to do so.** Melvin and Dingle do not give evidence and do not directly deny they fabricated evidence. Instead, the Smith conviction helps to conceal their crime and justify the fit-up: their defence against corruption charges is based on allegations that police believed Silcott *"committed at least one and probably two murders"* and that he *"was capable of suppressing evidence which might implicate him and, in particular, of terrorising witnesses."* (*Daily Telegraph*, 21 July) Detective Superintendent Eric Brown who led the Smith investigation testifies for Melvin and Dingle to say that Silcott is a dangerous man.

The defence also produces statements from **14 anonymous witnesses claiming they are too scared to testify against Silcott.** A number of these statements have already been thrown out at the Blakelock trial. One of the statements is from 13-year-old Jason Hill. Justice Hodgson dismissed it as "fantasy" and condemned the police mistreatment of Hill. Like Silcott, Hill is not asked to testify in the Melvin and Dingle trial. This court waste is now being recycled as anonymous statements. *"The real mystery is* *how the Crown and the judge, after days of secret hearings in chambers, can have allowed the policemen's lawyers to use these statements at all, let alone with the preamble that their authors were too frightened to give evidence."* (*Observer*, 31 July) Would anonymous statements have been allowed as part of the defence if the defendants had been Black men on trial accused of fitting up police officers for murder rather than police officers on trial, accused of fitting up a Black man for murder? Is the fact that the police consider the victim of this miscarriage of justice dangerous, justification for them breaking the law by falsifying evidence and perjuring themselves in court?

27 July

Silcott comments: *"The case was turned into a retrial of me."* Most of the press coverage backs the policemen: *"It is sad no-one would believe a DCS [detective chief superintendent] with 30 years' service who had investigated major crime since 1972 with no allegations of perjury made against him."* They report the effect on Melvin: *"The decision to charge began two and a half years of trauma for him and his wife."* (*Daily Telegraph*) Few question how the police officers can have been found not guilty of fabricating evidence when this was the reason the Court of Appeal decided that the Blakelock conviction was *"unsafe and unsatisfactory"*. Who else could have done it?

1 August

When Melvin and Dingle are acquitted of fabricating evidence against Silcott the Police Federation spearheads a campaign in the media to try to get Silcott's compensation withdrawn. This campaign runs over several weeks. The *Daily Mail* runs a week-long series of articles, with headlines like: *"ANALYSIS OF THE RELENTLESS PROCESS OF CANONISING A KILLER. HOW STICKS THE PICKPOCKET BECAME W. SILCOTT, MARTYR AND POLITICAL PHILOSOPHER."*

Another says, *"Metropolitan Police Federation chairman, Mike Bennett described the award as a 'slap in the face for victims of crime'"* and said **'he would be calling for a meeting with Home Secretary Michael Howard to discuss the award . . .'"**

One editorial says, *"Outrage upon outrage. Shame upon shame. The Silcott scandal grows worse by the day. . . . What is deeply disturbing in all this is the utter inability of our judicial system to understand the depth of public disgust."*

2 August

Johnson, another Police Federation official, is quoted as saying: *"**The lunatics are running the asylum.**" (Daily Mail)*

Reports that Silcott may get £250,000 compensation from a civil action he is taking against the Metropolitan Police for wrongful arrest and conviction, appear in the media to fuel outrage against him. Mike Bennett comments: *"I hope Scotland Yard fights this . . . If he wants money out of the police, we want the truth out of him. He should be questioned in court about what he was up to on the night. We are also of the opinion that convicted murderers should not be allowed to give interviews in prison." (Daily Mirror)*

3 August

*"**Winston Silcott is black, looks threatening** in some photographs and is a convicted murderer of a man called Tony Smith. **He is hated and feared by many for these reasons** . . . We are scandalised that he is receiving compensation for his quashed conviction for the PC Blakelock murder . . . **Silcott's blackness** works in his favour, too, of course [to get compensation] . . . I am tiring of the **bulbous-eyed photos** of Silcott. Perhaps the Earl of Snowden could take some new ones. He has always made a speciality of difficult subjects." (Evening Standard)*

4 August

Sir David Calcutt who decided to award compensation to Silcott is attacked in the press as *"a pillar of aloof establishment arrogance"*. He defends his decision straighforwardly: *"For me this is in no way a difficult case . . . he was in custody when he should not otherwise have been."* He says that in deciding the amount, he took into account a dossier of press coverage: ***"the publicity surrounding the conviction was of the gravest kind, and the abuse of Mr Winston Silcott and his family was grave.***

He was portrayed as a monster who exercised a rule of terror over the residents of Broadwater Farm. As a result his family were vilified by press coverage, abused and harassed at their homes and places of work. I accept that there was a comprehensive destruction of Mr Silcott's and his family's name in the national consciousness." (Independent)

Mary Silcott comments *"The money is nothing for him with all he has had to bear. No payment in the world could ever give back this family or Winston our self-respect."* Her son has been acquitted but he continues to be portrayed as *"the guilty man"*. Compensation is spent by Silcott on securing housing for his family and making a contribution to the Legal Aid Board.

Hardly anyone questions the impropriety of this police/media campaign. They continue to discredit Silcott without any reference to the miscarriage of justice for which the police have been shown to be responsible.

5 August

One police authority at least is critical of the Police Federation. *"The Police Federation has made a bad error of judgement in attacking the compensation paid to Winston Silcott . . . In the last year Humberside Police Authority has retired 14 officers following injury and on average they received a lump sum of £23,854 and a pension of £8,000, index-linked for life . . . Police authorities pay generously to officers retiring with injuries. The Police Federation should acknowledge this and publicly support the compensation payment to Winston Silcott who was incarcerated for a murder he did not commit, a fact the police seem unable to accept."* Ian Cawsey, Chair, Humberside Police Authority, *Guardian* Letters.

7 August

Or is it worse than that? **"One Scotland Yard source said recently: 'He is an animal. I don't care if he is guilty or not. You should be glad he's in jail for the sake of your mother and your sisters.'** " (Independent on Sunday)

16 September

Terry Hoffman, the doorman at the party, is interviewed by DI Norris and DS Clark. Hoffman is forthright in saying that when he first entered the room where the fight had happened his attention is first drawn to Silcott because he sees blood on his face and thinks his throat has been cut. This is despite attempts by Norris and Clark to get him to change his story. The interview is recorded secretly, and the Home Office refuses to disclose either the tape or transcript to Silcott's lawyers.

5 October

On the anniversary of PC Blakelock's death the Police Federation protest that Silcott has been changed from a high security Category A prisoner to a Category B prisoner in a more open prison. Again they act as if Silcott is serving a sentence for Blakelock, not Smith.

November

DCS Graham Melvin leaves the Metropolitan Police three months after being cleared for fabricating evidence against Silcott.

26 November

Although the Police Federation often invoke the name of Mrs Blakelock she has not initiated the witch-hunt against Silcott. At the time of Silcott's conviction for the murder of her husband she *"rejected any suggestion of restoring capital punishment. 'What good would it do? Would it bring my husband back? No, it wouldn't.' "(Independent,* 20 March 1987). When Silcott is acquitted she comments that if Winston Silcott was innocent, then *"someone is guilty . . . If he [Silcott] is innocent and has been in prison, that is wrong, but I feel that one day justice will be done." (Daily Telegraph)*

1995

7 February

Legal action by Adrian Clarke and Ed Rees, Silcott's barrister, forces the Home Office to disclose the transcript of Hoffman being interviewed by two police officers. The transcript shows that the police officers tried to get Hoffman to change his story. Clarke complains to the Home Office and demands that no other witnesses are interviewed without a solicitor present.

14 June

Clarke writes to the Home Office asking that the Home Secretary reconsider his decision of 19 January 1994 refusing to refer Silcott's conviction to the Court of Appeal. He submits further new evidence including the following statements:

Junior Bryan knew Anthony Smith as his brother's friend and a member of the Yankees which *"used to rob people and intimidate people in the community . . ."* Bryan saw Smith, Jones and Nelson *"behaving aggressively"* towards Silcott. He *"**saw Tony Smith with a knife in his hand** and also the tall man [Wayne Jones] who was with him. I then noticed that Winston had a knife."* Bryan says that he has *"never been asked to provide a statement in this case, neither by Silcott's solicitors nor by the police."*

Derek Henry saw Smith trying to provoke a fight and both Smith and Jones had knives.

Michael Jarrett says *"When Tony [Smith] paused in the doorway I saw that he had a knife in his hand . . . He walked towards Winston Silcott, and **he made a lunging motion with his hand towards Winston's face** . . . Winston put his hands up to block the knife and people started screaming. . . . **I saw blood coming from somewhere on Winston's face** . . . I was not contacted by the police to give a statement . . . **I was not contacted by anyone, not even Winston's Solicitors . . .** "* There is also an earlier undated statement taken by Christopher where Jarrett — Christopher's personal friend — says, *"At no time did I see Winston holding a knife."* This could lend credence to Silcott's statements that Christopher was actively manipulating the evidence to make it consistent with the defence Christopher advised Silcott to put forward. Jarrett's later statement confirms Silcott's version of events.

27 October

Silcott could be eligible for parole in 1996. But Home Secretary Michael Howard in whose hands Silcott's appeal rests, is reported as saying that he would never agree to free Silcott. (*Evening Standard*) Silcott's behaviour in prison is as good as that of men serving life sentences who are granted parole. For what conviction is he being held, Smith or Blakelock?

November

The Legal Aid Board withdraws legal aid for the civil case which Silcott is taking against Melvin and Dingle after representations are made by solicitors for the police. Legal aid is later reinstated after Silcott's solicitors appeal.

1997

March

The Criminal Cases Review Commission (CCRC) is set up to review "miscarriage of justice" cases. By now it is established in the public mind that the police and courts are not always to be trusted, and therefore that when a convicted prisoner says he is innocent, there is a reasonable chance that he may in fact be innocent. Silcott's case, along with all cases currently to be reviewed by the Home Secretary, is referred to this new body.

14 April

Mike Bennett, chairman of the Police Federation, is quoted as saying: *"We are seeking legal advice to see if it is possible to get legal aid for PC Blakelock's family, who would seek both to get a stay on any damages in his [Silcott's] case against the Metropolitan Police and to launch a separate action in conjunction with PC Blakelock's death . . . It is time someone took a stand. Silcott is running the show at the moment. I would like to see public opinion mobilised to see legal aid used properly, for the underdog."* (*Times*)

Just as Silcott's case is about to be considered by the CCRC Bennett says, *"He [Silcott] is constantly making waves for the*

[Blakelock] family and **causing problems. We would like him to have some problems of his own for a change.** *It is about time the public knew the truth and this is one way of it coming out."*

12 May

A freelance journalist complains to the BBC about their cameraman calling Silcott *"an animal"* on a vigil by miscarriage of justice campaigns outside the appeal hearing of the Bridgewater Four. He asks *"what balance can people expect if on such an occasion, they are met by such offensive and provocative remarks by a member of your staff?"* The BBC replies condemning the cameraman's behaviour. A policewoman is also overheard referring to the Blakelock case: *"How can they defend [Silcott] after what he has done?"*

18 July

Professor Leonard Leigh, the CCRC Commissioner in charge of reviewing Silcott's case, gives his preliminary report and concludes *"we are unlikely to refer this case to the Court of Appeal."* Clarke and Rees submit a response which is being considered.

25 July

Mike Bennett objects to a reception in honour of Silcott's mother and father which Black Women for Wages for Housework hold jointly with Legal Action for Women and Payday men's network: **"Why is it certain members of the black community only want to help criminals — and murderers to boot?"**

In response to the Commission saying they are unlikely to refer Mr. Silcott's case to the Court of Appeal, Bennett says: *"To be implicated in the violent deaths of three people and be convicted of one either makes Silcott the unluckiest man on the planet or a violent criminal —* **I choose to think** *he is a violent criminal."* (Haringey Independent)

* * * * *

Or is he is a man who has been the victim of a vendetta by police who expect that there are those in the Establishment to defend them whatever they do? In fact, previous miscarriages of justice show that those who already have convictions, as Silcott did for Smith, are most likely to be the targets of police fit-ups, as in the Blakelock case. Bennett of the Police Federation *"chooses to think"* that one conviction proves another conviction, that is, that you are guilty because you have been guilty on a previous occasion. This is neither justice nor the law. Unfortunately, in this case at least it is the police.

In *every* miscarriage of justice, the police have stuck with the view that those found not guilty on the evidence are guilty regardless of the final verdict of the court. Keeping Silcott inside has great practical, symbolic and political value for the police. If Silcott is not guilty of Blakelock then they have never got anyone for the killing of their fellow officer. (This has been the situation with *every* miscarriage of justice.) The police seem therefore to be committed to the view that he must stay inside on some other pretext; because if Silcott is innocent then the police are guilty not only of fitting him up but of never catching those responsible for the murder of PC Blakelock. This is bad for police morale. Can commanding officers expect the respect and obedience of their juniors when they are unable to catch those responsible for the murder of a fellow officer?

The Smith-Blakelock connection by dates

22 Dec 1984   Anthony Smith dies.

16 Feb 1985   Winston Silcott is arrested and charged with Smith's murder; and remanded in prison.

31 May 1985   Silcott is released on bail.

12 Oct 1985   Silcott is arrested for the murder of PC Keith Blakelock and is held on remand from this date.

15 Oct 1985   Widespread press coverage of Silcott's arrest for Blakelock.

3 Feb 1986   Silcott goes to trial for the murder of Smith while on remand for Blakelock. The jury is given police protection and armed police ring the court. Top police officers attend court including those involved in the Blakelock case such as DS Melvin and DI Dingle later tried for fabricating evidence against Silcott in the Blakelock case.

7 Feb 1986   Silcott is convicted of the murder of Smith. The prosecution mentions that Silcott is on remand for the murder of Blakelock.

21 Jan 1987   Silcott goes to trial for the murder of Blakelock.

19 March 1987   Silcott and two other men are convicted of the murder of Blakelock.

March 1987   The tabloids and some of the "quality papers" run a vilification campaign against Silcott which also mentions the Smith case.

16 March 1988   Silcott's appeals in both the Blakelock case and the Smith case come up one after the other on the same day before the same judges. The appeal for Blakelock is rejected and predictably so is the appeal for Smith.

25 Nov 1991	Silcott and the two other men are cleared of the murder of Blakelock after the ESDA test proves that Silcott's statement has been altered and must have been fabricated by the police.
Feb 1994	Silcott is given compensation for the Blakelock false conviction. The Police Federation attacks Sir David Calcutt for granting compensation and demands that the money should be withdrawn.
Aug 1994	DS Melvin and DI Dingle are cleared of fabricating evidence against Silcott in the Blakelock case. (No one else is ever charged.) DS Eric Brown, an officer in the Smith case, testifies on their behalf, that Silcott is a dangerous man. Silcott is never called to testify about what happened to him at the police station and what he knows about the false statement Melvin attributed to him. Another media vilification campaign which quotes the police follows.
July 1997	As Silcott's case for the murder of Smith is about to be considered by the CCRC, Police Federation chairman Mike Bennett says: *"He [Silcott] is constantly making waves for the [Blakelock] family and causing problems. We would like him to have some problems of his own for a change . . ."*

Niki Adams
24 January 1998

Legal Action for Women

Crossroads Women's Centre PO Box 287 London NW6 5QU
Tel: 0171-482 2496 minicom/voice Fax: 0171-209 4761

Sir Frederick Crawford DL, Chairman
Criminal Cases Review Commission
Alpha Tower
Suffolk Street Queensway
Birmingham B1 1TT

23 October 1997

Dear Sir Frederick,

We understand that you are considering evidence about the case of Winston Silcott. We submit for your attention a chronology of events from those leading up to Winston Silcott's murder conviction for the death of Anthony Smith to his current application for the case to be referred to the Court of Appeal.

As an anti-sexist, anti-racist women's legal service we do not often involve ourselves with the cases of men. Since we started in 1982 we have focussed on helping grassroots women who have little or no access to legal advice and who are more likely to be denied justice. We are probably best known for having helped two women in 1995 to bring a successful private prosecution for rape after the Crown Prosecution Service dropped their case. The private prosecution was the first of its kind in England and Wales and resulted in a serial attacker being sentenced to 11 years.

We were asked by Black Women for Wages for Housework to look at the case of Winston Silcott. They had been working for some time with Mr Silcott's family and especially with his mother, Mrs Mary Silcott, whose health is poor. No doubt you are aware that families of prisoners, in particular mothers and other women, do the painstaking and soul-wrenching work of keeping families together, visiting loved ones and attending to what needs they can, striving to ensure they have adequate legal representation, and campaigning for their release when they have been the victims of a miscarriage of justice.

The women at the Centre — which is a base for rape victims, women with disabilities and other vulnerable women — are extremely concerned about police hostility to anyone who believes in Mr Silcott's innocence. In July 1997 Black Women for Wages for Housework held a reception for Mrs Silcott who, in the face of what Sir David Calcutt called the "comprehensive destruction of

Mr Silcott's and his family name in the national consciousness", has carried the unenviable burden of campaigning for the truth to emerge. The police response to the reception quoted in the local press is very worrying: "Why is it certain members of the black community only want to help criminals and murderers to boot." We hope that our support for Mrs Silcott and her son will not make women at the Centre who are already vulnerable, targets of abuse or worse.We thought it was important to submit the enclosed because in our experience it is often difficult to have a full understanding of the facts of a legal case unless they are presented in context. It is only too easy to miss or misunderstand crucial aspects of a case, especially if evidence comes from people whose character may be in doubt and who belong to sectors of society whose words and actions are more likely to be mistrusted by those in authority. Yet character or sector must not be allowed to determine who gets justice.

We hope that our chronology will help shed light on the tragic events which engulfed Winston Silcott and his family as well as the families of Anthony Smith and Keith Blakelock. We trust that you will give it your unbiased attention.

Yours sincerely,

Niki Adams

Criminal Cases Review Commission

Chairman: Sir Frederick Crawford DL

Alpha Tower
Suffolk Street Queensway
Birmingham B1 1TT

Ms Niki Adams
Legal Action for Women
Crossroads Women's Centre
PO Box 287
London NW6 5QU

Tel: *0121 633 1800*
Fax: *0121 633 1804*

DX: 715466
Birmingham 41

27 October 1997

Our ref: 00279/97

Dear Ms. Adams,

Thank you for your 23 October letter concerning the review of Mr Winston Silcott's case by the Commission, and for the two attachments to it. I have read them carefully and have passed them on to Professor Leonard Leigh, the Commission Member working on the review.

When he is ready, Professor Leigh will submit his findings to a committee of at least three members of the Commission. They will take the final decision on whether or not to refer the case to the Court of Appeal. It is therefore very important that any new arguments or evidence supporting the contentions made in your letter and its attachments should be communicated to Professor Leigh as soon as possible.

I greatly appreciate receiving your letter, and hope that the case can be brought expeditiously to a conclusion.

Yours sincerely,

87

As from: **21 Church Street, Kingston, Jamaica**

November 12th, 1997

Legal Action for Women,
Crossroads Women's Centre,
P.O. Box 287,
London NW6 5QU

Dear Sisters,

Re: Winston Silcott

I write to give my wholehearted support to your campaign to re-open the case of Winston Silcott.

As Chairman of the Broadwater Farm Inquiry (1986 and 1989) I was acutely aware of the irrational prejudice which had spread like a poison against Black people in Broadwater Farm generally, and against Winston Silcott in particular. I interviewed Winston and recall him speaking eloquently about the effect on him, even in prison, of being "demonised" and thus being unable to assert his own human personality.

Our second report declared our belief that Winston was innocent of the Blakelock murder. Years later the Court of Appeal accepted that he had indeed been framed.

The Anthony Smith conviction seems now to be highly questionable and there are strong indications, as set out in your chronology, that this was a case of reasonable and legitimate self-defence.

Please convey my greetings to Winston Silcott and to his family. On my next visit to England I would like to see him again.

Yours sincerely,

LORD GIFFORD Q.C.

LG/tf.